ARTHUR BRYANT

RESTORATION ENGLAND

COLLINS

ST JAMES'S PLACE, LONDON

First published as
' The England of Charles II '
1934

© *Arthur Bryant Revised edition* 1960
Reprinted edition 1961
Printed in Great Britain
Collins Clear-Type Press: London and Glasgow

In Memory of
George Townsend Warner

Who could so watch, and not forget the rack
Of wills worn thin and thought become too frail,
Nor roll the centuries back
And feel the sinews of his soul grow hale.

v. SACKVILLE WEST, *The Land*

naturally, I set about to devote a year to a shorter work
that should epitomize such knowledge as I had gleaned

INTRODUCTION

THIS BOOK was written as the sequel to a long and, for me, very happy experience. It followed ten years' work on the Shakerley MSS.—a large collection of late seventeenth-century domestic letters, concerned mainly with the lives of Cheshire, Lancashire and Welsh country gentry, yeomen farmers and merchants, but comprising also much correspondence from London, Oxford and almost every other English county and city. For a decade it was my habit to transcribe twenty or thirty of these letters every evening. As a result, I found myself living as it were, two lives—one in our own century and another in an earlier one. The lives of these long dead folk, over whose shoulders I looked nightly, became for a time as real to me as those of my own contemporaries.

When I had finished writing my first two historical books, *Charles II* and *Samuel Pepys, The Man in the Making,* I decided to devote a year to a shorter work that should epitomise such knowledge as I had gleaned of how our ancestors lived in the reigns of Charles II and his immediate successors. This work appeared a few years before the war and was destroyed by the

Luftwaffe when its publishers' premises were burnt with the entire stock of the book. It has now been re-issued after a lapse of a quarter of a century in a revised edition and under a new name.

What is set out in it is a visit to a far country. That country was called England—the land we now inhabit but then occupied by our great-great-great-great-great-great-great-grandparents. Yet it is not so far from us but that a very old man living to-day might in his infancy have set eyes on another veteran who had seen one of its survivors. I have tried to depict that country as those survivors knew it—the feel and sense of it, its sights, sounds and even smells. In my first chapter—which, strangely enough, has been made the subject of a musical Suite [1]—I described the journey to London from Dover as contemporary foreigners experienced it; thereafter I have taken a number of different facets of daily social life—life in the capital, the family round, religion and worship, the means of livelihood, and the system of government, national and local—as experienced by ordinary people in the course of their everyday lives. I have left to others, like Sir George Clark and Dr. David Ogg in their broad studies of English 17th century history and Professor Basil Willey in his *Seventeenth Century Background,* the discussion of philosophic, political and theological ideas then forming in the minds of exceptional men, though probably little perceived by the ordinary English man

[1] Hubert Clifford, *A Kentish Suite,* (Oxford University Press).

and woman at the time. Mine is the common or garden, though I think, living England.

The chief source of the book was the as yet unpublished Shakerley MSS. But it was based, too, on every book and manuscript used by me in preparing my biographies of Charles II and Pepys. As the book, though a bye-product of scholarship, was written for the ordinary reader rather than for scholars, I have made no attempt to compile a bibliography but have merely added an appendix of references to the principal sources quoted.

To two great historians, Dr. G. M. Trevelyan and Dr. Andrew Browning, both of whom have enlarged our knowledge of late Stuart England and both of whom gave me generous help and criticism in writing this book, I should like once more to record my debt.

Wincombe, 1960   *Arthur Bryant*

CONTENTS

13

LIST OF ILLUSTRATIONS

ILLUSTRATIONS

CHAPTER I

APPROACH TO ENGLAND

" For all that I have yet seen, give me old England."
Edward Hyde, Earl of Clarendon

ONE usually approached her from the French shore, travelling in the packet-boat from Calais. The drawbacks were much as to-day, only they were more acute, for not only was conversation in the boat apt to be interrupted, as one disgusted traveller put it, by the disorder which those who are not accustomed to the sea are subject to, but such interruption was more prolonged. Adverse winds might hold up the mail-boat for several days, and it was fortunate if this delay occurred in harbour rather than in mid-Channel. In reasonably fair weather the crossing took seven hours.

Even before landing the sensitive traveller was made aware of the island, for if the wind blew from off her cliffs scents of thyme and sheep on the uplands were borne out to sea. Other scents, too, for the little town of Dover was as innocent of the art of sanitation as any in Europe. Nestling beneath her castle, she presented an inviting appearance, which closer acquaintance modified. Both castle and harbour works were much decayed, and the shingle was constantly drifted by storms into the fairway, so that on more than one occasion the Mayor was forced to summons reluctant householders with shovels to the beach for the customary labour of clearing the harbour. And once—it was in 1662—a government office in London was aroused from lethargy by the arrival from the storm-beleaguered town of a missive fearfully endorsed: "In haste, post haste, or all's lost; port, town and people."

Landing was attended by formalities—by the officers of the Customs with prying eyes, by those of the Castle on watch for undesirable entrants (a constant succession of whom were lodged in its dungeons and who, aided by bribery, almost as constantly escaped), and, in the case of very distinguished visitors, by the Deputy Master of Ceremonies sent down from London to do the honours.

For more ordinary mortals welcome was accorded by the younger and lazier inhabitants of the town, who, leaving their games or their loafing, accompanied them to their inns with such affronts as they deemed appropriate to the species of foreigner before them. Of these the most common was the cry of "A Monsieur, a Monsieur," accompanied by a certain mocking and dandified gait; it was best to accept this with a smile, for opposition to the island proletariat quickly brought out its more quarrelsome traits, and jeers would then give way to angry growls of "French dogs" and threats of worse. For the "Come to Britain" movement had no counterpart in the England of 1660; her people expected foreigners to take them as they found them.

Not that they were unreasonable. Those of the more educated class were not averse to criticism; in fact, as they sat around the newcomer over the inn fire they invited him to express his views on their customs and character, and even seemed to take pleasure in hearing the truth; only if it were adverse they showed plainly by their laughter that they did not believe it. They appeared to have plenty of leisure and to be in no particular hurry about anything, spending much of their time drinking, taking tobacco and talking, disapprovingly for the most part, about the Government; nor, for all this apparent laziness—and even the poorest were slothful—did they seem to suffer the flagrant destitution so noticeable in a continental town. And when, after the night's stay, they presented the bill, it was obvious that they were accustomed to gentlemen with well-lined purses.[1]

From Dover the traveller climbed the hill and rode over the downs—" a pleasant champaign country with the sea and the coast of France clear in view "—to Canterbury. There was wide choice of transport. Those in a hurry might gallop the twelve miles in an hour's time on the excellent post-horses in which the island abounded, for these English, though lazy in the ordinary concerns of life, were rapid in travelling; the very country people rode to market " as it were for a benefice ". Or, if one shirked the heavy post-horse charge of threepence a mile (with an extra fourpence for the guide at each stage), and did not mind being made a little sick, one could travel more slowly in a wagon drawn by six horses and directed by a gentleman with a whip who walked beside carrying on a perpetual interchange of personalities with his passengers.

The sights of the road revealed England. Gentlemen's coaches, with six horses drawing them and much colour and gilt of emblazonry, travellers, carriers and drovers passing and repassing, country-folk going to market, and in the fields or on the open downs beside the grass highway, haymakers and shepherds at their business. Occasionally there would be some special excitement: a royal courier riding post, or, if it were assize time, the splendid inconvenience of being jostled out of a narrow lane by the coaches and horses of the judges and lawyers pressing forward to the next circuit town.

Beyond the road the landscape stretched into blue horizons. " The country and the grass here," wrote one who saw them for the first time in 1670, " seemed to me to be finer and of a better colour than in other places." Trees were everywhere, stirred to life by sea-breezes that blew perpetually across the island, carrying with them clouds which gave changing lights and shades to every contour. And in the weald beyond the downs there were orchards of apple and cherry, so many that from an eminence it looked as though the whole land was given over to forest. Here, too—and this was unlike the greater part of the country, which was still open—there were enclosures with quickset hedges surrounding the meadows; parks, too, with smooth parterres and bowling-greens before houses which, though inferior in grandeur to the châteaux of France, had with their homely timbering and long peaked roofs a trim and intimate dignity of their own. The general effect was that of a planted garden.[2]

Of the weather one was made conscious from the first; for it was much as it is to-day. All that could be predicted of it for certain was that it would never be for long the same. Summers of rare loveliness, when the fruit and corn ripened to a bumper harvest and July flowers were out in May, and Christmases bright with snow and holly, lived as now in the consecrated memory of old men; more usually the climate showered down its variegated blessings with humorous inappropriateness. "A verie tempestious slabby day" would be succeeded by a night of "brave moonshine"; "a good misling morning" by an afternoon gale; and a hard frost by "a monstrous great thaw" that sent everyone unexpectedly skidding down the streets. One January it was so fine that dusty roads were haunted by flies and the rose-bushes were full of leaves— "glorious and warm, even to amazement, for this time of year"; in the same May, after two months of almost continuous rain, the bishops declared a fast; only when the time came the weather had changed to drought, so that they were forced to compromise according to Anglican wont by keeping the day half as a fast and half as a feast. Yet though they hated the white fogs which haunted the country ditches and crept even into the towns, foreigners praised the general salubrity of the climate: there was pure air, plenty of wind, and an absence of anything that enervated. And the soft moisture of the atmosphere gave the land ever-changing beauty and colour—the blues and greys and silver whites that enchanted every horizon.[3]

Canterbury was the first town reached. At a distance, its cathedral rose majestic above the surrounding walls; nearer at hand it was seen, like the town itself, to be in that decay which, since the days of the Reformation, had befallen the cathedral cities of England, and which the deliberate desecrations of the Commonwealth men in recent years had only intensified. Still the general air of ruin was qualified, as in all things English, by a certain pleasant and intimate charm. There were ancient prebendal houses of crumbling stone set in gardens of blossom and fresh green, and in the narrow streets of the city itself the houses, so low that occupants of middle height were forced to stoop perpetually, nestled together till their eaves almost touched. To a foreigner it seemed remarkable that all the windows were glazed and mostly without shutters; those of the lower rooms had curtains and iron bars for privacy and safety, and those of the upper casements which opened in the middle, throwing at night a delightful air of candle-lit intimacy on to the street below. Another peculiarity were the bay windows, which, set in little angles and projections of the houses, enabled a householder to overlook the street in both directions without being himself observed. And behind each house, which was thus in itself a small castle, were gardens and meadows; for *rus in urbe* was the English rule.[4]

Leaving Canterbury on the Faversham road, the traveller entered a land of apples, hops and cherries. High two-wheeled carts drawn by oxen, bearing hops for the local maltsters or Kentish pippins and russets for the Medway and Three Cranes Wharf, herds of red bullocks with crumpled horns from the Weald pastures, and troops of labourers with scythe and sickle tramping for refreshment to the next village, showed the agricultural interests of the neighbourhood. Indeed, Kent was a kind of agriculturist's Mecca, with its great hop gardens, its orchards of cherries, pears and apples, its tidy habits of cultivation, and its high wages. Its only drawback for the labourer, who in harvest-time could earn as much as two shillings a day (almost double what he could hope for elsewhere) was its notorious agues. But of these the traveller was as yet unaware.

Faversham, a long, straggling town, encompassed the road for over a mile. Beyond the town, coast and road ran for a time within sight of each other, until from the higher ground west of Sittingbourne the traveller

23

caught the gleam of the Medway. A few miles later he entered the twin towns of Chatham and Rochester. Here were the King's naval arsenals, with lanes of storehouses going down to the water's edge, and a main street which stretched for half a league along the Medway until it crossed it by a stone bridge, adorned by a parapet of iron balusters set there by the authorities to catch suicides and hats.[5]

After Rochester the way divided. Here experienced travellers left the main London high road through Dartford, and bore riverwards to Gravesend. In doing so they were wise to seek each other's company, for the road passed over Gad's Hill, notorious since the days of Falstaff for its robberies. Here on a summer's dawn in 1676 a highwayman on a bay mare robbed a gentleman as he came over the brow of the hill; then, setting spurs to his horse, crossed the ferry to Tilbury (where the delays attendant on tide and a leisurely waterman kept him champing for nearly an hour) and hastened through the Essex lanes to Chelmsford and thence over the downs to Cambridge and Huntingdon, where he rested his horse. An hour later he was mounted again and, galloping up the Great North Road, miraculously reached York the same afternoon, where, after changing his clothes, he repaired to the bowling-green and, singling out the Lord Mayor, made a small wager with him on the fortunes of the game, being careful to ask the time as he did so. All of which subsequently proved an irrefutable alibi, and not only earned the highwayman, whose name was Nicks, a triumphant acquittal but a private interview with His Sacred Majesty King Charles II, who was entranced by the whole story and endowed his prudent subject with the sobriquet of " Swift Nicks."[6]

At Gravesend, a little snug town of watermen's houses, one took the ferry for London. Here outgoing ships were forced to anchor for a last visit from the Customs officials, and there was always a fleet of vessels riding in the road. With the tide in one's favour, one could reach London in four hours, either by wherry or, if one chose to be less exclusive and more economical, by the common tilt boat which carried up to sixty passengers at eightpence a head. One had one's money's worth, not only in the passage, but in the sights—fleets of colliers beating up the river with Newcastle coal, Barking smacks with mackerel, sailing under such clouds of canvas that it seemed they must at any moment upset, hoys from Deal and Sandwich bringing the produce of Kent to London, and merchantmen bound for the Indies or Mediterranean. As one proceeded, the chalk-pits and marshes near Gravesend gave way to almost continuous villages and yards busy with ships' carpenters making vessels to take possession of the watery realms which the Navigation Acts were giving England. For those who loved the sight of busy mankind it was the most beautiful river in Europe.

At Woolwich travellers crowded to the port gunwale for a statelier sight, where in the deep water against the shore the King's gilded yachts lay against the wall of the dockyard. A mile beyond, under the trees of its sloping park lay royal Greenwich, with its old, rambling palace, sadly plundered in the late troubles, lying in ruins, and on the lawns that stretched before the Queen's House, which Inigo Jones had built under the hill, a new palace of white stone rising by the waterside. Then, in a moment, one was in the grey, windswept waters of Long Reach, with one unbroken arsenal stretching along either shore—the greatest shipbuilding centre in the world, save, perhaps, the yards at Schiedam by Amsterdam. Yet within living memory what was a continuous street of buildings along the water had been a lonely tract of marsh, broken only by the gallows on which condemned pirates had been wont to hang till three tides had covered them. And so, at the bend by Limehouse, one came to London. Before lay the Tower, and the many-arched, house-crowned bridge, and the Thames flowing out to meet the sea between a hundred spires and a hundred thousand roofs.[7]

CHAPTER II

THE CAPITAL

AROUND the London of 1660 there were still walls, thirty-five feet high in some places, with bastions and gates such as King Hal had ridden through on his return from Agincourt. But the suburbs had long outgrown the city's medieval confines and were spreading tentacles in every direction over the fields. At the Restoration, London housed anything from half a million to six hundred thousand, or about a tenth of the total population of the kingdom, and stretched from Westminster to All Hallows, Barking, and from Shoreditch to St. George's Fields. But there were as yet no buildings north of St. James's Park or west of St. Martin's; St. Giles was still in the fields, and grass meadows fringed the inns along the northern side of Holborn; Southwark was bordered by marshy dikes, and Kensington, Islington and Hackney were country villages. Less than half a century later the population numbered a million, and the houses stretched from Blackwall to Chelsea. Throughout Charles II's reign, despite the destruction wrought by the fire, "this great and monstrous thing called London" grew perpetually. It is hard, therefore, to say exactly where one entered it, but the traveller knew by the old formula, " *So soon as the coach was got upon the stones.*"[1]

For it was then that the rattle began. Of wooden and iron wheels rumbling on cobbles, of apprentices standing before every shop bawling, " *What d'ye lack?* ", of hawkers crying, " *Lilly white vinegar,*" and " *White-hearted cabbages,*" and " *Kitchen stuff, ha' you maids* "; and, as the warm months drew on and rich folk wished themselves on their country estates, " *Cherry Ripe,*" " *Peas,*" and " *Fine strawberries.*" There were custardmongers (the forerunners of our costers) hawking apples; old clothes men, and small coals men with sacks of Newcastle cobbles on their backs, milkmaids rattling pails and intonating, " *Any milk here?* ", tinkers with loud " *Have you any brass pots, iron pots, skillets or frying-pans to mend,*" and mouse-trap men with " *Save alls* " and " *Buy a mouse-trap, a mouse-trap, or a tormentor for your fleas?* " One sensed the context of these incitements to commerce by their music rather than by their words; bythe lilt and rhythm of

> Here's fine herrings, eight a groat,
> Hot codlins, pies and tarts,
> New mackerel I have to sell.
> Come buy my Wellsfleet oysters, ho!
> Come buy my whitings fine and new.[2]

Nor were these the only sounds. In narrow streets crowded with coaches and carts, traffic control tended to be a matter of vocal adjustment " till the quarrel be decided whether six of your nobles sitting together shall stop and give way to as many barrels of beer." Every nobleman's coach was preceded by a footman calling on the proletariat to make way for his master, a claim which the draymen and the drivers of hackney coaches were quick to dispute. These last, which waited for their fares in ranks at street corners, were to be had at a shilling a mile or eighteen pence an hour. To travel in them was to be involved in frequent turmoil. There were traffic blocks which, lasting sometimes half an hour, set whole streets swearing and shouting; accidents when wheels came off or bolts broke so that the horses went on and the passengers remained stationary; Jehu-like incidents, such as set splashed and endangered pedestrians screaming with rage or brought down in some narrow thoroughfare the hanging wares from the hooks outside the shops.* ³

Even at night the noise of London persisted, the constable and his watch brawling with midnight revellers, the watchman's cry of " *Past one of the clock and a cold frosty windy morning*," and the sounds which bespoke the agricultural undertakings hidden behind London's urban exterior, like that " damned noise between a sow gelder and a cow and a dog " which woke Pepys up one sultry summer's night. For the

---

* So, as one fare recorded, " The butchers stopped the horses, and a great rout of people in the street, crying that he had done him 40s. and £5 of hurt; but going down, I saw that he had done little or none; and so I give them a shilling for it, and they were well contented."—*Pepys' Diary*, 15 Dec. 1662.

country's capital was still rural at heart, and the rich earthy smell of the fruits and beasts of the home counties lay about it.[4]

One did not only hear London, one smelt it. The sanitation of the day was Oriental in its simple grandeur, and its effects, comparatively innocuous in a country village, were appallingly noticeable in the metropolis. Rivers of filth coursed down the centre of each street, and, at the time of the emptying of slop-pails, the passer-by nearest the wall had cause to be grateful for the overhanging stories. Around the city stretched a halo of stinking, steaming lay-stalls, haunted by flies and kites, while in the densest quarters of the city the grave-yards, piled high above the surrounding ground, re-peopled themselves. Even on a spring evening, when the air was full of scents of sap and blossom from the trees that shaded every court and alley garden, the citizen taking the air on the leads of his house was sometimes driven indoors by (to use Pepys's graphic phrase) " the stink of shying of a shitten pot." The most cultured, however nice in their own tastes, were utterly innocent of public sanitary sense, the refined Lord Guilford installing a pump to drive the piled ordure from his cellar into the street.[5]

Public conveniences there were none. The polite would step aside to an alehouse, those less so to the street wall. Mrs. Pepys, taken ill at the theatre, uncon-cernedly went out into Lincoln's Inn Walks and " there in a corner did her business." Even in their houses our ancestors did not always employ the houses of office that the richer among them tucked away in cellar or on leads; Pepys himself occasionally made use of the bedroom chimney. All this must seem revolting to modern taste, but is necessary to correct the popular impression derived from the "My Lady in her lavender beds" view of the past.[6]

It explains also why our ancestors regarded London as such an unhealthy place. Country mothers wrote anxiously to their sons bidding them have a care of the close, crowded air, and Members of Parliament, when the end of the session released them to their country homes, recalled with horror the smells descending into the House from the small apartments adjoining the Speaker's Chamber. Small-pox and fevers, and more periodically bubonic plague, haunted the town, subsequently spreading all over the kingdom. They were the price England had to pay for the wealth which its growing capital made for it.[7]

Other signs of Mammon's watching presence attended the city. Between it and the sky visitors frequently noted a pall of smoky vapour, arising from the furnaces of the brewers, soap-boilers, and dyers, who, unhindered by State or Corporation, carried on their trades in its heart. Evelyn, the most fastidious observer of his day, wrote indignantly of the "horrid smoke which obscures our churches and makes our palaces look old, which fouls our clothes and corrupts the waters." In winter this coal vapour sometimes de-

scended on the streets in a blanket of fog, so that
" horses ran against each other, carts against carts,
coaches against coaches." Yet we who are accustomed
to far worse pollution will be mistaken if we take these
contemporary plaints too seriously, for usually the rays
of the sun reached the trees and flowers of the city
courts without hindrance, and the Thames, for all its
unseen load of filth, still sparkled brightly.[8]

For the reverse of the picture is true. If the London
of Charles II was dirty, it was also beautiful. Colour
and the pomp of life, moving in gilded majesty, came
back with the King; these things, in which all shared,
were the visible signs of an inward and spiritual grace.
The streets were full of bright garments, ruffling and
sparkling in the wind. Pepys clothed his footboy in
green lined with red, and went abroad himself in a
summer suit of coloured camelot, with a flowered
tabby vest, very rich, and gold lace sleeves. And on
May Day, when he drove in Hyde Park in his new
coach, the horses' tails were tied with red ribbon, the
standards were gilt with varnish, and all the reins were
green.[9]

The background of this pageantry was before 1666
the medieval city which Chaucer had seen in his
youth and in which Shakespeare had loved and worked.
The houses were framed in oak, with walls of lath
and plaster, and their overhanging stories were painted
and heavily carved. Compared with Paris the city
spread outwards rather than upwards; the buildings

were low and in the better quarters inhabited by only one family apiece, save round the Court and the New Exchange, where furnished rooms and lodgings could be had at easy rates. But in the outer suburbs, in hovels pent together of weather-boards smeared with pitch, the poor were crowded together in indescribable congestion.

Along the southern side of the Strand were the palaces of the nobility. These had gardens running down to the Thames, with private stairs on to the water. Other great mansions, standing in parks and gardens, were scattered round the western outskirts— Bedford, Wallingford, and Burlington Houses, and the vast mansion which Lord Chancellor Clarendon built himself in the fields beside Piccadilly and was never suffered to inhabit. More manageable in size were the substantial houses which rich merchants built and country magnates, in attendance at Parliament or Court, rented. Such was Sir Nathaniel Hobart's fine new house in Chancery Lane, " near the ' Three Cranes ', next door to the ' Hole in the Wall '," with " a very handsome garden with a wash house in it," carrying a rental of fifty-five pounds a year.[10]

Rising above the houses of rich and poor alike were the churches. The sky of the city, as one saw it from the southern bank, was pierced by over a hundred spires, and, dominating all, the nave and tower of St. Paul's. The spire of the cathedral had fallen many years before, and the nave had been half ruined by generations of decay and the depredations of the Interregnum. Cromwell's troopers had used it as a stable, and there had been an unsuccessful attempt to sell part of it as building material for a Jewish synagogue. Yet it was still, after St. Peter's in Rome, the greatest church in Europe.[11]

The streets between the crowded buildings were narrow, cobbled with egg-shaped stones, with posts at the sides of the broader thoroughfares to protect pedestrians, and rendered fantastically crooked by the uneven frontage of the houses. Above them painted signs, projecting on creaking iron branches, proclaimed to an illiterate age the addresses of their occupants— the " Three Pigeons " in Great Queen's Street, or the " Crooked Billet " " over against Hill, the Quaker cook's, upon the Mall Bank, Westminster." Behind the streets were courtyards and lanes, sometimes giving access on to a hundred others, sometimes ending in nothing, like that " blind alley, on the backside of Mr. Trice's house, just at the close of the evening," where Dryden's wild gallant was wont to make his rendezvous. Here, too, were gardens with fruit and flowers, and here the innumerable stables which the coaches and horses of the capital required. " Now for the stables," wrote a London friend to Sir Ralph Verney. " I have my choice of two. One is in Magpie Yard. There is a pond on the yard to wash the horses in and very good water. It will hold four horses, and the hay loft will hold four loads of hay. There is bins

34

for oats. They say they are very honest and civil people; Judge Atkins's coach has stood there this fourteen years. Now there is another at the "Red Harp" in Fetter Lane; 'tis one turning more beyond the "Magpie", but it has the same conveniency. The "Magpie" is sixteen pounds a year, if they lodge a man; the other I can have for fourteen pounds." Those with cars to garage in modern London may be interested by these homely details.[12]

On winter nights the principal streets were lit until ten or eleven by lanterns placed at regular intervals, and, more spasmodically, by the uncertain efforts of householders who were expected between the feasts of All Saints and Candlemas to expose their light to the street—a civic obligation often compounded for or evaded. More useful were the linkboys who waited at every corner with torch and lantern to light travellers home. These poor urchins—recruited from the ragged company of homeless strays who lodged in doorways and disused penthouses—assailed the passer-by with cries of "Do you want light?" Grander citizens like Pepys, who went out to supper with the wench carrying a lanthorn before him, provided their own street lighting.[13]

At intervals London was lit by a brighter illumination. The houses were built "as if formed to make one general bonfire," and, whenever a careless householder supplied a spark and the wind was in the right quarter, they obliged. The parish authorities, with leather buckets, hatchets and iron crows for removing thatch, the enthusiastic Lord Craven and his amateur fire-fighters, and the fire-engines of the early insurance companies (who, however, with dawning commercial instinct confined their efforts to the houses of their own clients) did something to keep this perpetually recurring nuisance within bounds. But in September 1666, with a summer gale blowing from the east after long drought, they met their match. In four days a third of the city perished, including the cathedral, the Guildhall, and eighty-four churches.[14]

This destruction, far from holding up London's growth, stimulated it. The new brick houses that arose in the devastated areas were so much more handsome and commodious than the old that property owners whose houses had not been burnt became anxious to rebuild. Moreover, many, who had gardens round their houses in the old London, recouped themselves for their losses by building houses and shops where formerly had been grass and trees. Mr. Swithin's spacious garden by the Royal Exchange reappeared as Swithin's Alley, with twenty-four houses upon it, and what had been the stable-yard of the " King's Arms " in Coleman Street became in the new London Copthall Court. This example of building on open spaces was followed in the unburnt portions of the town, and one by one the great houses of the nobility disappeared, to be replaced by squares and terraces bearing the names of their former owners. Of the great palaces along the Strand only three remained by the end of the century—Somerset House, the Savoy (itself divided into apartments), and Northumberland House—while Essex, Norfolk, Salisbury, Worcester, Exeter, Hungerford and York passed into a new chapter of London's topographical nomenclature. And since, while the town was rebuilding, the dispossessed shop-keepers opened their booths on Moorfields and other public open spaces outside the city, these latter also tended to disappear and grow into streets and squares; for where London had once encroached it never receded.

Yet the old divisions remained. The new houses rose on the same lines as the old, the strength of the foundations and walls undestroyed by the fire making it difficult for them to do otherwise. The merchants and shopkeepers went back to their old haunts: Thames Street once more stank of oil, tallow and hemp, the goldsmith bankers rehung their signs in Lombard Street, mercers and ladies' tailors span their webs in Paternoster Row, and drapers and booksellers in Paul's Churchyard. And the fashionable folk of the West End continued to inhabit the stately porticoed houses of Covent Garden and Lincoln's Inn Fields (both spared the fire), though before the end of the reign there was a tendency to migrate farther west to the new houses which Lord St. Albans had laid out on his property to the north of St. James's Palace. For still, in the new London as in the old, birds of a feather flocked together. Even the street-vendors returned to their ancient haunts, and nuts, gingerbread, oysters and night-caps were sold as of old from the barrows by Fleet Bridge at the foot of Ludgate Hill.[15]

The wares which Londoners purchased came to them through the great markets—meat from Hungerford and Queenhithe, fish and coal from Billingsgate, cloth from Blackwell Hall, herbs from Covent Garden and the Stocks Market, horses and livestock from Smith-field, and fish, butter, poultry, bacon, raw hides, leather and baize from mighty Leadenhall. The shops were small, consisting generally of the open door and front downstairs room of the house in which the shopkeeper's family and apprentices lived and worked. But though the multiple shop was unknown, the bazaar already flourished. Great ladies with their husbands and " servants " flocked to the New Exchange in the Strand, which, with its rows of shops along double galleries of black stone, conveniently adjacent to the fashionable quarter of the town, had long ago out-distanced its Elizabethan rivals, the nave of St. Paul's Cathedral and the old Royal Exchange in Cornhill. And here were those elegant young women, the semp-stresses and milliners of the Exchange, who, with their ogling eyes and pretty chirpings of " Fine linens, sir, gloves or ribbons," made gentlemen customers buy more than they had intended, and who sometimes, unless they have been sadly maligned by their con-temporaries, were not averse to selling their persons as well.[16]

All this business required refreshment, and it was easily to be had. Eating-houses ranged from grand taverns like the " Sun " in Fish Street, or the " Dolphin " (beloved by Pepys) in Seething Lane, to little cook-shops where one might feast on a chop of veal, bread and cheese and beer for a shilling, or buy a joint or sirloin of roast ready cooked for consumption at home. A common mode of dining was to take the " ordinary " at the long table of a tavern, each man contributing his share of the conversation and paying his club. At one such Pepys and a friend had " very good cheer for 18*d.* a piece . . . and an excellent droll, too, my host, and his wife so fine a woman and sung and played so well that I stayed a great while and drank a great deal of wine." A month later, revisiting it, the same diner-out had another tale to record of " great wrangling with the master of the house when the reckoning was brought, he setting down exceeding high everything."

Places of purely liquid refreshment were innumerable; had one tried to count all the ale-houses between the " Hercules Pillars " by Hyde Park Gate and the " Boatswain " in Wapping, one might have counted for ever. In these, men of all classes congregated to smoke, drink and talk—much to the astonishment of foreigners, who could not accustom themselves to the way in which they left their work at all hours of the day for this purpose. Later in the reign, the place of the ale-house was partly taken for the middle classes by the coffee-house. This was a novel institution and a great place for the latest tattle of Church and State, derived as likely as not by the loquacious master of the house from the barber or tailor of some courtier's valet. So popular did the coffee-houses become and so seditious the conversation therein, that the Government was forced to issue proclamations against them and subject them to the same licensing restrictions as their rivals the ale-houses. Out of the coffee-house evolved the club, already, in an informal and not too exclusive way, in its genesis.[17]

In public buildings (other than churches) London was not rich. There was the Guildhall and the Royal Exchange, where merchants met for news and business, the Customs House and the Navy, Victualling and Pay Offices, the Old Bailey, and the prisons of King's Bench, Fleet, Bridewell and Marshalsea, and the Halls of the City Companies. There were also seven beautiful, though for the most part crumbling, gates. And just outside the city walls was the Temple, which escaped the Great Fire, only to enjoy a private fire of its own in 1677—rendered legally memorable by the pedantry of a young barrister who, in the midst of flames, sternly warned the Duke of York and his fellow fire-fighters that they were rendering themselves liable to an action for trespass. That he was subsequently hit over the head with a crowbar does not detract from his professional glory.

One other important London building escaped the

View of London from Southwark by Thomas Wyck

The frozen river

e Temple, 1684

Fire and frost on the Thames, 1666 and 1677

fire—the Tower—thanks to the forethought of Pepys and Admiral Penn, who fetched up the men from the royal dockyards to fight the flames. The old Norman fortress was the chief landmark of eastern London and a great resort for country visitors. Here were the Mint, the Ordnance, the national archives, and the royal armoury, and here, displayed behind an iron grill, the crown jewels which Blood, the Irish outlaw, attempted to steal in 1670. There were also lions. These, named after the kings of England, were much gaped at by hordes of country cousins and children, and shared their captivity with a number of mangy leopards and eagles.[18]

Other sights were Westminster Hall, the Court at Whitehall, the tombs and effigies in the Abbey, the lunatics at Bedlam, and the penitent prostitutes who beat hemp under the lash at Bridewell. There were also the wooden figures that struck the quarters on St. Dunstan's Church to the delight of a crowd of country fellows daily congregated in rapt attention before them, and the monsters of the animal world who were nearly always on show in street or tavern— the bearded woman of Holborn, the calf with six legs and a topknot, and the rhinoceros, on which the enemies of Lord Chief Justice North so irreverently declared they had seen him riding. Grander spectacles were the regular events of the London round—the Lord Mayor's Show and its pageantry by land and river, the drills of the City Trained Bands in Artillery fields, and the great September saturnalia of Bartholomew Fair.[19]

But finest of all the sights of old London was its river. For nearly eight miles it bordered the houses, nor, so dependent were its citizens upon it, did the town at any point stray far from its shores. There was no embankment, but the buildings came down to the waterside, where a succession of slippery stairs joined the city lanes to the life of the water. This winding blue canal was the Londoner's highway and the ceaseless background of his life. It was governed in theory by the Lord Mayor and his Water Bailiff, whose jurisdiction as Thames Conservator stretched from Staines Bridge to the Medway. In practice it was ruled by a corporation of jolly, swearing Wapping watermen, who brooked no competition and whose ribaldry was proverbial; though what it was they shouted to the western bargemen about the women of Woolwich which made them so mad we shall never know, and perhaps it is as well. For fear of them, though at any hour of the day coaches, drays and cattle were mingled in profane confusion on London's single bridge, no other bridge could be built, and the King, who called them his nursery of seamen, supported them.[20]

It was by these one was greeted as one approached the waterside. From the wooden benches that fringed the stairs there started up a clamorous multitude of grizzly Tritons in sweaty shirts and short-necked doublets with badges on their arms, hallooing and hooting out, " Next oars " or, more elaborately if their prospective clients were of the black-coated fraternity, " Scholars, scholars, will you have any hoars?" Their boats were of two kinds—sculls with one rower, and the faster " oars " with two, in which one could travel with a favourable tide from one end of London to Westminster in a quarter of an hour.

The boats were not uncomfortable. Passengers sat on cushions and had a board to lean upon. But there was no covering save a cloth spread over a few rough hoops in the stern, generally soaked before there was time to raise it—a fact which caused the Secretary of the Admiralty to have his open boat converted into a barge with a cushioned cabin, painted panels and windows that slid up and down in sashes like those of a coach.[21]

The bridge was one of the wonders of Britain. Guarded by piles or " starlings " to protect the stone-work, it stood on eighteen arches and was crowned by a double row of shops and houses, six stories high. Nervous passengers, frightened by the foam and roar of its cataracts, were wont to land at the " Old Swan " on the northern bank and rejoin the boat below the bridge. Save that one was apt to get " soundly washed," shooting the rapids was not so bad as it looked; in flood-time one could take up haddocks with one's hands as they lay there blinded by the thickness of the waters.[22]

The language of the watermen was a greater wonder

RESTORATION ENGLAND

than the bridge itself. It was a point of honour among
them to exchange badinage of the coarsest kind with
every passer-by: those acquainted with the adven-
tures of Sir Roger de Coverley in a later age will
remember how this worthy gentleman, crossing to
Vauxhall Gardens, was hailed as an old put and asked
if he was not ashamed to go a-wenching at his years.
And this was mild abuse for a Thames waterman.
Sometimes they met their match: a boatload of
Lambeth gardeners, it was held, could return them as
good as they gave and more. Knowing clients took a
hand in the game themselves and flung back gibes at
passing boats; it almost seemed to them as though they
were aiding the course of navigation. [23]

To those who took the foul language and rough
humour of the watermen as part of the game, the river
was full of delight. There were the gilded barges of
the King and the nobility, with gorgeous liverymen,
the long, shallow boats that bore malt and meat to
feed London from the upper reaches, the picturesque
and very dirty vendors of fruit and strong waters, who
with wheedling shouts brought their unlicensed skiffs
alongside. When the weather was hot, one might pull
off one's shoes and stockings and trail feet and fingers
in the water; at flood-tide see the water coursing over
the mill banks opposite Vauxhall and boats rowing in
the streets of Westminster, or at low-tide watch a
daring boy wading through mud and pebbles from
Whitehall to Lambeth. On moonlit nights the river

44

took on a peculiar enchantment, and the primitive, literal minds of our ancestors turned to bawdry, or as naturally but more decently to the sweet, wistful, half-innocent, half-wise music which was the crowning beauty of the age. They were in many things still children, these forbears of ours, whose ghosts even now pass and repass across the surface of the river, and it is as children as well as men that they must be judged. And, like children, they had their fears and their horrors: " troubled to-day," wrote the Clerk of the Acts of his Majesty's Navy, "to see a dead man floating upon the waters, and had done (they say) these four days, and nobody takes him up to bury him, which is very barbarous."

The river served for pastime as well as business. Boys and young men swam in it naked, barristers like Roger North kept yachts on it to while away briefless days* racing the smacks and hoys, and shopkeepers, adventurers, and poets alike sought its cool breezes on burning summer evenings. Pepys was always using the river for recreation. He would " on a sudden motion " take up his wife and his maids in a frolic

* " There was little remarkable in this day's voyage, only that I, with my friend Mr. Chute, sat before the mast in the hatchway, with prospectives and books, the magazine of provisions, and a boy to make a fire and help broil, make tea, chocolate, etc. And thus, passing alternately from one entertainment to another, we sat out eight whole hours and scarce knew what time was past. For the day proved cool, the gale brisk, air clear, and no inconvenience to molest us, nor want to trouble our thoughts, neither business to importune, nor formalities to tease us; so that we came nearer to perfection of life there than I was ever sensible of otherwise."—*North, Lives*, III, 32.

and with cold victuals and bottled ale sail down to Gravesend to see the King's ships lying in the Hope, or, more usually, take the evening air as far as Greenwich or the Chelsea " Neat House." At Barn Elms ladies and courtiers came on June afternoons with bottles and baskets and chairs to sup under the trees by the waterside. Higher up beyond Hammersmith and Putney were gentlemen's villas and gardens and pleasant villages. Small wonder that the seventeenth-century Londoner loved his river and went abroad on it whenever he could to look on " the sun, the waters and the gardens of this fair city." [24]

He could take his pleasure if he chose in other ways. As the working day began before dawn, and most well-to-do folk left their business not long after mid-day, there was plenty of time in the long summer afternoons for recreation. For those whose views were not too rigid there were the two licensed theatres, with their circular tiers of boxes to which admittance cost four shillings or more, their half-crown pit and their upper galleries where, for a shilling, footmen and other humble but by no means silent spectators could obtain admittance. The King's Theatre was in Drury Lane, and the Duke of York's or Opera House in Lincoln's Inn Fields. Though decidedly smart, the theatres were informal and friendly; ladies and gentlemen, much to the horror of foreigners, sat side by side in the boxes, and sometimes, it would appear, on one another's knees. In the pit women selling oranges shoved and

wheedled their way between the spectators; while the
King and Queen with Castlemaine and the great ladies
of the Court sat without state in the boxes above. In
all this the licensed playhouses were the microcosm of
a new age, which demanded fare less rough and
imaginative, better mannered and more intimate than
had been afforded by the older pre-Commonwealth
drama. From their little picture stages, with their
green baize coverings, their scenery screens " embel-
lished with beautiful landscapes," their tall wax candles
and velvet curtains, dainty actresses, with impudent
alluring ways, looked down on bewigged, approving
gentlemen. [25]

For less sophisticated folk there were still the unlicensed theatres of the Red Bull and Sadler's Wells,
where a good deal of rather extravagant noise and
ranting amid rough surroundings could be enjoyed at
a moderate charge. Far wider in popular appeal, sup-
pressed in name under the Commonwealth though
never quite in fact, were the Bear and Bull Gardens,
and the cock-pits in which the proletariat (and its
betters) took their rough pleasures. Pepys has left us a
picture of one of their cock-fights: " After dinner . . .
directed by sight of bills upon the walls, I did go to
Shoe Lane to see a cock-fighting at a new pit there . . .
But Lord, to see the strange variety of people, from
Parliamentmen to the poorest prentices, bakers,
butchers, brewers, draymen and what not; and all
these fellows one with another in swearing, cursing

and betting. I soon had enough of it, and yet I would not but have seen it once, it being strange to observe the nature of these poor creatures, how they will fight till they drop down dead upon the table, and strike after they are ready to give up the ghost, not offering to run away when they are weary or wounded past doing further, whereas a dunghill brood . . . will, after a sharp stroke that pricks him, run off the stage, and they wring his neck off without more ado, whereas the other they preserve, though both eyes be out, for breed only of a true cock of the game." The more squeamish Evelyn, at the Bear Garden, saw a bull toss a dog into a lady's lap many feet above the arena; saw also two dogs killed and the show end, amid applause, with an ape on horseback.[26]

Through all this rough texture ran a thread of pure beauty. Perhaps it was because the fields were never far away; trees invaded the streets and squares; there were gardens lurking behind the houses, and nightingales in Lincoln's Inn. And since the fields were so near, the recreations of the citizens were still in part rural. On May Day the milkmaids with garlands and silver on their pails, danced down the Strand with a fiddler playing before, while Nell Gwynne, in smock sleeves and bodice, stood at the door of her lodgings and watched them go by. All round the town were the green places to which the Londoners repaired whenever their occasions allowed them: Hyde Park, with its balustraded ring round which the coaches drove the rich and fashionable; Moorfields with its mulberry trees; the meadows and milk of Hackney for the apprentice, the farthing pie-houses of Hoxton for the mechanic, and Epsom waters for "*Steeple-hat*" the burgher and his mincing lady. One might sit in one's coach and drink ale at a tavern door, or take a morning mess of cream and sillabub at "The World's End" in Knightsbridge, or visit the Mulberry Gardens—a pretty place by moonlight, and a vast contrast, with its "rascally, whoring, roguing sort of people," to the trim 19th century Buckingham Palace which in due season, rose in its place. Farther afield lay Kensington's grotto, the cherries of Rotherhithe, and the cakes of Islington; the Jamaica House at Bermondsey—where Pepys's maids ran races on the bowling-green; or, best of all, wooded Vauxhall, with its spring blossoms, where one could listen to the nightingale and other birds, and "here fiddles and there a harp, and here a Jew's trump, and here laughing, and there fine people walking."[27]

Yet if the London of Charles II seems rural to us, it was metropolitan enough to our forefathers. Such a one would visit it in an Easter term to sample its towny joys—to the destruction of tarts and cheesecakes—to see a new play, buy a new gown, take a turn in the park. He would sup at the "Hercules Pillars" in Fleet Street or at the sign of "Old Simon the King" —or, if he wished to be very fashionable, at the new French house in Covent Garden, Chatelin's, with its fricassees, ragouts and salads, its music and gay company, and its unforgettable bills. And everywhere for his delight were sociable little taverns in blind corners, " The Trumpet," " The Sugar Loaf " or " The Green Lettuce "; " The Old House " at Lambeth Marsh, where Pepys on his unlawful occasions wheedled the wives of his naval subordinates; the little bawdy house behind the House of Lords, where he went to drink wormwood; and the fair, frail ladies whom Mother Temple and Madam Bennet in Drury Lane or Moorfields vended to all and sundry.[28]

CHAPTER III

THE UNIT OF LIFE

THIS was London—the rich foam on the surface
of the national brew—but England was the country.
And in those days, when the total population did not
much exceed five millions, there was plenty of space
in it—elbow-room for liberty and solitude for thought
and unsullied imagination. The French ambassador,
travelling westwards, was surprised to see how empty
it was, passing, in a distance of thirty leagues of fine
land, very few villages and scarcely a soul on the road.
Yet how lovely this open, lonely land was, and how
rich its people in everything that made life worth
living! " I wish I were with you a little in the sweet
country," wrote town-tied Mrs. Shakerley to her
Cheshire neighbours. In Devon the folk clotted their
cream with sugar to crown their apple-pies, and, in
the fields beside the Ouse in Huntingdonshire, the
milkmaids bore home their pails with music going
before them. In that county, so rich was it in corn,
it was the custom, whenever a king of England came,
to meet him with a hundred ploughs.[1]

Here in the country quiet the old ways of life persisted. Pepys, walking on Epsom Downs, far from any house or sight of people, found an old shepherd reading the Bible to his little boy. Parson Moore of Horsted Keynes did his shopkeeping by barter, receiving a box of pills and sermons in return for a ribspare and hog's pudding, and in remote parts of Lancashire boon services were still unsuperseded by rents. The colliers of the Tyne rowed merrily by verdant flats and woods, with trumpeters and bagpipes making music in the stern, and west of the Pennines the country-people went bare-footed, leaping as if they had hoofs. Rich and poor alike talked and spelt in the dialect of their own county, Cheshire Mrs. Dobson writing to tell her husband:

> "I leve here tow and twenty milke cous and a boll, three big hefers and a boleke and seven which are yer old bes; and one boll calfe which runs upon one of the coues and seven other calves which are this year rered, and one fat tegg."

It was a world of country squires and parsons, of yeomen and cottagers and ragged, cheerful squatters, making their own wares and their own pleasures after the manner of their ancestors. For " that great hive, the city," its vices and graces, country-folk had nothing but pity. To cousins there imprisoned they sent vast cheeses and pies of game: " there was two very fat geese, eight wild ducks, and eight woodcocks, and in the box a pair of stockings," in one such that Lady Shakerley sent her son in London. " When I came home," wrote Robert Paston, " which is the sweetest place in the world, I found my children and Mrs. Cooper pretty well, and she and the gentleman are taking their pleasure to see an otter hunted in the pond." It was so all over England.[2]

The unit of this country life, out of which England sprang, was the family. It was the greatest of all the national institutions—greater than King, Church or Parliament. These had been laid low by Civil War and only recovered by Restoration; the family had remained as it was through all the troubled times. It remained so, too, after the Restoration, when some text-book historians would have us suppose that because there was licence in Whitehall the whole moral life of the nation was poisoned. But the doings at Court made small difference to the domestic life of manor, farm and cottage.

For marriage in the seventeenth century was built on sturdy foundations. That insubstantial but romantic passion which the moderns call " being in love," had usually small, if any, part in its genesis, though that deeper affection which arises out of mutual com-panionship and long-suffering kindness was often its reward and attendant. At the Court, where young people of either sex were congregated with little to do, the modern manner of falling in love was already the vogue—the effect, as Pepys said, " of idleness and having nothing else to employ their great spirits upon." From such a leisured and cultivated society

53

the poets were mostly drawn; hence arises the phenomenon that to read of seventeenth-century love from
the pen of the Court poets is to fancy oneself in our
world, and from those of the letter writers in quite
another.

Ordinary people, of course, fell in love, but they did
so in a very matter of fact way. Marriage was looked
on as a necessary settlement for life and was associated
with the disposal of property. It was usually initiated
by those who had the present possession of such
property. Rich parents, therefore, began to plan their
children's marriages early, sometimes as soon as they
were born. It never occurred to them that there was
anything inhuman in this, but merely an early settlement on a dear one's behalf of one of life's most difficult
undertakings. So kind and virtuous Sir Ralph Verney
described "a young wedding between Lady Grace
Grenville and Sir George Cartwright's grandson,
which was consummated on Tuesday by the Bishop of
Durham; she is six years old and he a little above eight
years old, therefore questionless they will carry themselves very gravely and love dearly."

Nothing could strengthen a great family more (in
days when the family was all-important) than a rich
and influential marriage. When, as rarely happened,
an elder son was so undutiful as to kick over the traces
and choose for himself the defrauded father was justly
indignant. " Sir," wrote Lord Cork to his heir, " I
am informed that you are so miserably blinded as to

incline to marry, and so with one wretched act to undo both the gentlewoman and yourself and . . . to dash all my designs which concern myself and house." On the other hand, though to choose for oneself against one's parents was unforgivable, few parents expected a son or daughter to marry anyone to whom he or she felt an active aversion. A right of veto was nearly always allowable, such as John Verney used when he had his prospective bride paraded up and down Drapers' Garden for an hour that he might see " if there were nothing disgustful about her."³

The marriage of a daughter was not a profitable business. Nor was it usually easy. Young ladies with fortunes of their own were, of course, readily disposable; " Sir Ambrose Crawley's daughters go off apace, but £50,000 ladies will never stick on hand." But no father or guardian would allow his son or ward to marry a girl, however charming or attractive, who did not possess a portion proportionate to his estate, and, in those days of large families, few young women could bring a great dowry.

In the correspondence of the time, therefore, the girls often present a somewhat pathetic picture: nervously anxious to marry and doomed to a life of dependence as companion to some rich relative if they should fail. " I think," wrote one young lady in despair, " my marrying very unlikely in any place and impossible in this." Shortly afterwards she made a runaway match with a penniless curate: anything, she felt, was better than being left an old maid. "I am not so much lost," she explained to her horrified relations, "as some may think, because I have married one who has the repute of an honest man, and one as in time I may live comfortably with."[4]

Far happier was the lot of a rich bachelor or widower disposing of himself. He had only to choose the most suitable of the many excellent matches offered him. "I hear you have buried your good lady long since," wrote one ardent matchmaker, "may it please your worthy sir to pardon my boldness herein, if it should please your Worship to have thoughts of another, to let me tell your Worship of a lady—a most truly virtuous, modest, maidengentlewoman—who hath neither father nor mother nor brother nor sister. She hath £400 a year besides much money; her £400 a year is free land of inheritance to give to whom she pleases: a more pious, modest gentlewoman is not to be found."[5]

Unless her friends made a careful settlement of her fortune before her marriage a woman was economically at the mercy of her husband. In a petition before the House of Lords against a Hertfordshire landowner a wife complained that she had brought him a portion of eight thousand pounds, and that, as soon as he had possessed himself of it, he had cruelly dismissed her servants, forced her to live in a wool chamber and finally turned her out of doors. It is just to add that in his reply the husband alleged that he had never received

56

The King on Horse Guards, 1685

The Tic

Dole, 1670

Longleat, 1675

that sum, that the lady lay in the wool chamber on her own account in order that she might dispose of his plate and jewels, that she had appropriated his money, refused his conjugal affection, and brought an armed and amorous trooper into his chamber to challenge him to a duel.[6]

All this made a marriage settlement a complicated business, particularly where a big estate was concerned. The legal advisers of both parties would write packets of letters and famous counsel in London would be feed, so that children and grandchildren unborn might be provided for and remote contingencies anticipated. Often months, and sometimes years, would pass before the final details were complete and the young people free to wed. In one case, at least, the latter took matters into their own hands and married before the legal formalities were completed, the father of the bride (who gained greatly by the bridegroom's impatience) writing to his discomfited opposite, " And to show you he is your own son, we had much ado to keep him from kissing his bride before matrimony was all read."[7]

Though occasionally, as in this case, genuine tenderness sprang up between the young people before the wedding, a conventional phraseology of courtship was de rigueur. They called themselves one another's servants and wrote such letters as young William Blundell with his father's aid wrote to Mary Eyre: " Oh! my most honoured dear Lady, how shall I count those

unkind hours that keep me from so great a joy? I told
you once before (as I hope I did not offend) that your
goodness hath cause to pardon what your virtue and
beauty hath done." The real love-letters of the seventeenth century were written not before but after
marriage. There are a few exceptions like those of
Dorothy Osborne. Forbidden to see her love, she
wrote to him: "I think I need not tell you how dear
you have been to me, nor that in your kindness I placed
all the satisfaction of my life; 'twas the only happiness
I proposed to myself, and had set my heart so much
upon it that it was therefore my punishment to let me
see that, how innocent soever I thought my affection,
it was guilty in being greater than is allowable for things
of this world." She waited for him for seven years and
had him in the end without breaking any of the com-
mandments of God or man.[8]

From courtship and the making of settlements one
passed into marriage through the ceremonials and
junketings of an English wedding. In the villages of
the west the bride on her wedding eve was locked
with her bridesmaids in her father's house, while the
bridegroom, with music before and all the village after,
marched through the street to claim admission, which
was treacherously effected by one of the bridesmaids
opening a window. In Northumberland the bridegroom leapt with the bride over the louping-stone at
the church door, and in the little wooden church of
Nether Peover in Cheshire a maid showed her right to

be a farmer's wife by lifting with one brawny arm the great oak lid of the Peover chest.

On the bridal day the company put on coloured scarves, love-knots and ribbons, and fine gloves and garters. These were also given by the bridegroom to his absent friends as tokens of remembrance: " A pair of green fringed gloves for my brother, white and coloured lace gloves for my sister, pink coloured trimmed gloves for Master Ralph, my coloured trimmed gloves for Master Munsey, white gloves trimmed with green for my little niece, and one of my wife's wedding garters for Master Ralph." At the wedding feast the sack posset was eaten and, when all were high-flown, the bride was undressed by her maids and the bridegroom by his male friends, the company coming up from their junketings below to see them to bed, scramble for ribbons and garters, fling the bride's stockings and draw the curtains on them. " We saw Sir Richard & his fine Lady wedded," wrote Edmund Verney, " & flung the stocking, & then left them to themselves, and so in this manner was ended the celebration of this Marriage a la mode; after that we had Music, Feasting, Drinking, Revelling, Dancing, & Kissing: it was Two of the Clock this morning before we got Home."

On the morning after the wedding the bride was woken by the town music, which assembled beneath her window to greet the first day of her married life. Sometimes she must have wondered what sort of companion had been given her: "I pray to God," wrote one bride, "I have got an 'onast religas man." It is pleasant to know that her faith was not misplaced. "She says that he is very loving to her," a friend testified, "and if she had married a Lord she could not have been more happy."

Honeymoon there was none, and for the first few weeks after marriage the bride had the comfort of still being surrounded by her own folk and friends. Then she passed into the possession of her husband's family, and became as much the daughter of her father- and mother-in-law as if she had been their own child. She was usually received with real love and kindness, for in the seventeenth century the tie of kinship was very strong and sacred.

So she came to her husband's or his father's house: "All the country sent her in presents, and when they come home they was met within three miles of the house with six score of the gentlemen and yeomen, and at Debenham all the women with garlands and flowers, and strewed them home to the house where my Lady and her company and her servants waited on her and the music followed her."[9]

Perhaps it was because there was practically no chance of divorce that the marriages made in this prosaic and homely fashion seem to have endured so well; it never occurred to bride or groom that the union they had made was for anything but life. In the narrow circle of the Court and the fashionable society of

and husband seems to grow brighter with the passage of years. "Dearest Heart," they are writing to each other long after the charm of youth had vanished; " as for this little groaning wife of my own," testifies William Blundell after half a century of buffetings bravely shared, " I think she will never fail me."[10]

Once married a woman had plenty to do. In this respect my Lady was as good as Joan, the village housewife. The management of a country house called for all a woman's energies. Invested with her châtelaine of keys, the squire's wife was made mistress of kitchen, brewery and buttery, storehouse and stillroom. It was her task to provide " wholesome and cleanly diet " for husband, children and household, to keep cows and poultry for dairy and larder, to see that the fish-ponds were stocked and the herb-garden tended. Under her charge was the great household which the smallest manor-house was forced to maintain in an age when public services were in their infancy, and even letters had to be fetched by a servant from the nearest post town. And in a large mansion the normal retinue of butler, cook, housemaids and scullions, laundry- and dairymaid, coachman, grooms and footboys, were reinforced by a whole regiment of retainers—an Auditor of the Revenue and a Receiver of the Rents, a Steward and a Gentleman Usher, a Chaplain and Clerk of the Kitchen, a Gentleman and Yeoman of the Horse, a Bailiff and perhaps even a Monsieur such as that " brisk, gay spark, that had been bred at Court as a page and

could dance, sing and play neatly on the violin"
whom Lord North delighted to keep at Kirtling and
who was such an object of dislike to the old gentleman's
relatives. And all these, besides the guests who came
and went perpetually, the lady of the house had to
feed.

Another occupation of a country gentlewoman was
to keep the recipe and herbal books which were among
one of the regular heirlooms of any substantial family.
In them she would enter not only recipes for dishes,
but more special directions for making preserves and
comfits for honoured guests, rose and lavender waters
for perfumes, and preservatives for the sick. A country
house in those days was a factory for all the best that
English life could offer, making its own food and drink
from seeding to brewhouse and kitchen, its own fuel
and candles, spinning flax and wool for clothing and
upholstery, and even curing feathers to make its own
mattresses and pillows. Of all this work the lady of
the house was priestess, and her maids her acolytes.
She had no need to spend her days on committees or to
busy herself with the machinery of government or
social reform. "I hear she looks to her house well,"
wrote Lady Hobart of her newly wedded niece,
"and grows a notable housewife and delights in
it."[11]

She was also a mother. The end of marriage was the
procreation of children, and nobody in those days
made any bones about it. "I hope," wrote one hus-

band, " that I shall yet live to see my little round wife come tumbling home to her brats with a brat in her belly." And parents were always praying that God would " fill the cradle with sweet brave babes." The prayer was generally answered. " Your mother," wrote a ruined cavalier to his son, " was well delivered of her tenth daughter (the thing is called Bridget), so that now you have had three sisters born in the space of 32 months. You may well think that is not the way to get rich." An unseasonable blessing in such a case, as one father observed, " but God's will be done."[12]

Among the upper classes, children were often christened after the royal family; there were many Charleses and Marys in the generation born between 1630 and the outbreak of the Civil War. Traditional family names were also popular; the constant succession of Geoffreys and Peters among the Shakerleys, or Ralphs and Edmunds among the Verneys is apt to be confusing. Sometimes, owing to the determination of parents to have at least one living descendant bearing a favourite name, the same name was given several times in a single generation—there were two Paulinas and two Thomases among the brothers and sisters of Samuel Pepys. The middle class and peasantry varied traditional English local names—the Christophers, Cecils, Michaels, Benedicts, and Agneses, Audreys, Dorothys, Ursulas, Eleanors and Priscillas of my own East Claydon—with Oriental names from the Bible—

Noahs, Ezras, Sarahs, and Judiths, and rarer and more distinguished Jeremiahs and Zurishaddais.

The Puritans were never content to be anything but better than other men. Surpassing the names of such simple Christian virtues as Comfort, Temperance and Charity, and even the more unusual Silence, with which one seventeenth-century girl was christened, they annexed whole texts from the Scriptures to describe and distinguish their children. Mr. Barebone, President of Cromwell's Parliament of saints, was christened " Praise God," his brother " If-Christ-hadst-not-died-thou-hadst-been-damned "; while twelve Sussex jury-men who appear on a county panel during the Inter-regnum do so as Accepted Trevor, Redeemed Compton, Faint-not Hewit, Standfast-on-High Stringer, Kill-sin Pimple, Be-faithful Joiner, Fly-debate Roberts, Fight-the-good-fight-of-faith White, More-fruit Fowler, Hope-for Bending, Weep-not Billing and Meek Brewer.

Christenings were great occasions, attended by much tipping or " vailing "—so much for the nurse and so much for the midwife—and by presents of silver cups and spoons for the new-born. Feasts of mince-pies, wine and christening cake were held below, while the gossips crowded upstairs to drink a caudle by the mother's bedside and admire the fine white satin clothes and quilt, embroidered with scriptural texts or sprays of flowers—the work of her waiting months. It was all very neighbourly and kindly, and there was a pleasant air over this, as over so many of our old celebrations, of ordinary people being happy over an ordinary event which none the less they found intensely exciting and significant.[13]

Few mothers of that age were too grand to nurse their own young. "I wish you could see me sitting at table with my little chickens one on either side," writes one great lady; "in all my life I have not had such an occupation to my content to see them in bed at night and get them up in the morning." Another paints her happiness in words that still glow like the colours from a painter's brush: "My boy is now undressing by me and is such pretty company that he hinders me so I cannot write what I would."

Bred on brown bread, cheese, and small beer (drunk from a cool stone jar, into which careful mothers sometimes dropped a little rhubarb), children were fortified against the many infantile diseases of the age and their even more terrible remedies. One parent, given to amateur doctoring, wrote of his little boy: "It seems to me that his brain is no little oppressed with phlegm or moisture: he spits exceeding much, and I think when he spits the most his memory is the most defective"; an issue in the arm, he urged, should therefore be made immediately. And a favourite cure for measles was to send the patient to bed with a live sheep.

The rod played an important part in infant well-being, even little girls being " swinged to some purpose to teach them civility "; for our ancestors, though they loved their children, were great believers in nursery discipline. Filial piety they regarded as the beginning of wisdom; and, remembering the size of their families, it was a belief which must have helped to make family life more bearable. It was the custom of the time—and a pretty one—for children to stand bare-headed in the presence of their parents, and on any important occasions to crave their blessing.[14]

Education began early. Life was too uncertain to prolong childhood unnecessarily; the sooner boys stood on their own feet and girls were safely married the better. The alphabet was taught from the horn-book—a printed page pasted on a small wooden bat, covered with transparent talc and framed in horn, which was attached to a child's neck by a ribbon from the handle. This instrument which could be bought for threepence, was quite as convenient for battledore and shuttlecock as for learning.

Theology was the first step in all seventeenth-century education. On its supreme need parents of every denomination from " Papist " to " Fanatic " were agreed. Catholic William Blundell composed long catechisms for his children, and Nonconformist Oliver Heywood called his little ones into his study for spiritual wrestlings and " sweet meltings." Our Anglican catechism is a reminder of the thoroughness of this branch of English education. The very alphabets were Biblical, one beginning:

In Adam's fall
We sinned all,

and ending ingeniously :

Zaccheus he
Did climb a tree
Our Lord to see.

While the girls were set to sampler work and the
arts of deportment and household management, the
boys, armed with goose-quill, slate and ink-horn
advanced against the first entrenchments of the Classics.
There was a particularly terrible and time-honoured
grammar for beginners, with the intriguing sub-title,
"A Delicious Syrup newly Clarified for Young
Scholars that thirst for the Sweet Liquor of Latin
Speech." The sweet liquor, however unwelcome, had
one advantage, that it gave youth the hard mental
discipline by mastery of intellectual difficulty which
tends more than anything else to make the human
mind "categorical and not wiggle-waggle." And
since a classical education was the lot of nearly all who
held governing positions in Church and State, the
community suffered perhaps less than it does to-day
from rulers without the power to make up their minds.

Leaving aside such prodigies as little John Evelyn,
who could, before his fifth year, besides asking many
astonishing questions in divinity, decline all the nouns,
conjugate the verbs, regular and most of the irregular,
and recite the entire vocabulary of Latin and French

primitives, the average of attainment was strikingly high. Classical thought permeated the culture of the English governing class. Thirteen-year-old Richard Butler, who had been brought up at home in the wilds of Ireland and was regarded as exceptionally backward for his age, read over Cæsar's *Commentaries* in Latin to his grandfather with the greatest ease. " You may find us now and then," wrote the latter, " up to the ears in Plutarch, in a hot dispute whether Alexander or Cæsar was the braver man, and perhaps within an hour or two this gallant young disputant will be up to the knees in the brambles, at the head of a whole regiment of pitiful tatter-maddions beating to start a hare."[15]

Boys designed for the liberal professions went to the local grammar or Latin school, where future squires shared the same benches with the cleverer village lads who were later to be their tenants and neighbours— a practice which prevented any social segregation of the ruling class from the rest of the nation.* An English country gentleman of the time of Charles II was seldom out of touch with the people he was called to lead; from birth to death he was constantly with them —played with them on the village green, shared the sorrows of the same cane and Latin grammar, and met them at markets and hare-huntings.

---

* The elder sons of the nobility, however, a small and very exclusive class, were mostly segregated from both their fellow-gentlemen (whom they regarded as much below them) and from the mass of their country-men, and were brought up by private and generally rather obsequious tutors. This was probably the root of much subsequent evil.

Yet the germs of our educational caste system were being sown. There were already a few private establishments kept exclusively for the sons of gentlemen, while certain of the old Latin schools had acquired so national a reputation that country squires were beginning to send their boys there instead of to the nearest grammar school. Foremost of these were Eton, Winchester—" the best nursery for learning for young children in the world "—and the great home of classical culture and royalism, Westminster, then famous as the scene of Dr. Busby's chastisements. A lady of Wales spoke proudly of her boy being " under the lash of Westminster School." (The regimen seems to have been successful, for in the latter half of the century, Westminster produced such a list of scholars, statesmen and prelates as few schools have equalled.) Another great London seminary was St. Paul's, which, before its ancient building perished in the Great Fire, nursed the youthful genius of Milton, Pepys and Marlborough.

Yet even at these larger schools there was still a wide measure of democracy; clever boys from country cottages would accompany the young squire and share his lessons at his father's expense, while the humblest citizen could still regard the great London schools as his children's birthright. And the system, though rough, was pleasantly informal and intimate; parents would send presents to their boys' schoolmasters, which the latter acknowledged in long, friendly letters. A charming example of the informality of the system exists in a letter of 1672, telling how Dr. Cromleholme (many years before the teacher of Samuel Pepys) received the poor protégé of a small north country squire at St. Paul's:

" Yesterday, Dr. Frankland went with myself and Mr. William Clayton along with the boy to Dr. Cromleholme, who readily gave the child, and us, a very free and welcome entertainment; and to be short he gave us order to remember his love to the boy's mother, and to let her know from him that he received her boy as his own, and that he willed as carefully of him as if he was his own, and that he will (by God's blessing) give him learning and send him to Oxford, and that he doubted not of friends to get him preferment there. He called up his wife, and said ' Sweetheart you must take this child as mine and yours,' which she denied not, but asked her husband who he was like; he would have her judge first, whereupon she said the boy was very like a brother of hers, and he concurred with her in the matter. He was very glad the boy was past the measles and the small pox. After we had drunk a glass or two of ale about, he placed his hand on the boy's head and blessed him saying, ' the Lord God Almighty bless thee, and not only give thee wisdom and learning, but his grace also.' "[16]

For most Englishmen there was no book-schooling save such as was given for a year or so in extreme youth (and soon forgotten) at the village dame's school. In the modern sense the majority of the population was illiterate. Pepys tells of a Mayor of Bristol who pretended to read a pass with the bottom upwards. Yet there was education for nearly all, and good

education at that. For it was education in craftsmanship and vocation, lovingly taught by father to son as
the best thing which he could give his child in days
when skill in a particular trade was almost as privileged
a thing as the property which the rich left their heirs:
a tailor's son became a tailor, and a boatman's a boatman. One virtue of this kind of education was that it
utilised the imitative instinct in children, since a boy
usually wants to copy the work of the grown men
around him. And it taught a child to do one thing
thoroughly (and that the trade which he was to follow
for the greater part of his days), and to take a joy in
doing so. The man who has learnt that has not only
mastered one of the main secrets of happiness, but is
educated. He has found his own strength in overcoming
difficulties and discovered that there is no such thing
as taking a short cut to avoid the inevitable. Such a
man has a truer sense of values than is given by a smatter-
ing of many branches of knowledge and a mastery of
none.

Culture in the widest sense came from the reading
of the Bible, whose effect on the permanent thought
and tradition of the nation it is hard to overestimate.
In the stricter sense of the word it was the prerogative
of the two Universities. Both played a great part in
the education of seventeenth-century England, and in
particular of its leaders.

At Cambridge, a borough of under ten thousand
inhabitants, there were two thousand five hundred

scholars in residence, and at Oxford, which was even smaller, three thousand. At both Universities the college system was already fully established, and, like much else of the period, was based on the local divisions of the nation. A Buckinghamshire lad was sent to Magdalen, Oxford, and one from Cheshire to Brasenose. Here he enjoyed the learning of a foundation which drew its revenues from the broad acres of his own shire, whose members spoke its still broader but to his ears inexpressibly dear accents, and whose Fellows were countrymen and friends of his father or patron. Between the college tutors and the magnates of their home county there was a great deal of pleasant contact: Westmorland Fleming of Rydal sent " venison pies and large tokens " for ale to the dons of Queen's: " If we had not been a great company of good fellows," they replied, " we should not have been able to get it spent, but we conquered it at last, and hope that His Majesty and yourself will be the happier for our remembrance." Sir Daniel and good King Charles must have been the better for such learned and liberal toasts.

Though few matriculated at twelve or thirteen, as in the past, boys went to the University early. Sixteen was the average age. With a dozen years of classical learning behind them, they already possessed the easy culture of men of the world. " I am sorry that you should have such a bad account of me," wrote one lad to a guardian who was bombarding him with querulous letters, " but must beg leave to think that they you should have it from are neither your friends nor mine. That I have not followed my studies as I ought to have done I confess with shame, but who is he that has? Where is he to be found? I would not by this argue myself comparatively studious, for such a way is odious to all, but really, sir, one of the greatest obstructions to my study has been your continual chiding of me."

The instruction given was mainly classical, though theology and, at Cambridge, mathematics, played an important part. But there was much else: at Oxford the regular course of studies prescribed by the Laudian statutes included Grammar and Rhetoric for the first year, Aristotle's *Ethics* and *Politics* for the second, and Moral Philosophy, Geometry and Greek for the third, while Bachelors before proceeding to the Magisterial degree were expected to study Geometry, Astronomy, Metaphysics, Natural Philosophy, Ancient History, Hebrew and Greek. Then as now the greater part of the work was tutorial, and founded on private reading. "My tutor reads to me once and sometimes twice a day in Saunderson's logic," writes an undergraduate in 1670. " In spare hours I read Lucilius, Flores, Sallust and such historians. I think I shall go into Hall next term to the Disputations." These were formal exercises in logic, derived from the metaphysical debates of the Middle Ages. Often they were mere strings of conventional questions and answers which, committed to paper and secretly concealed in their caps, were used by undergraduates at the Disputations for Degrees. They were called wall lectures, presumably because nobody listened to them except the wall.

Yet, like our present examination system, though riddled with absurdities, Disputations had their uses. They helped to give a shy lad self-confidence; " Your son is both frugal and industrious," wrote a college tutor, " but he wants courage and heart. I hope that disputing in the Hall will put briskness and metal into him." And they taught him to speak boldly and clearly, no ill accomplishment for one later to be set in authority. " Child," Edmund Verney warned his undergraduate son, " I pray when you speak in the Theatre, do not speak like a mouse in a cheese, for that will be a great shame instead of an honour, but speak out your words boldly and distinctly and with a grave confidence." This was in the spirit of the age.

Lectures as a form of instruction were on the decline. With the increase in the average age of undergraduates, dons were inclined to regard themselves as absolved from the schoolmastering side of their business and free to devote themselves, the best of them to scholarship and research, and the worst to idleness and tavern haunting. But the business of lecturing was not as neglected as is supposed. As late as 1684 a father wrote solemnly to an Oxford son, reported to him as having been absent from lectures: " It is a wrong to the society not to come to lectures, for if all others would forbear coming to them as you do, the lectures would

fall which are a support to the College, and so by degrees
Arts and Sciences and learned societies must dwindle
away, and so dissolve to nothing. I hope," he added,
" none of my posterity will ever be the *primum mobile*
of such a mischief to learning."

The University round was still fairly spartan. The
undergraduate's day began at dawn.* Chapel at six,
a breakfast of crust and ale and then to work. But the
taint of snobbery which was soon to transform the
national dividing lines from perpendicular and local
to horizontal and class, was already beginning to
poison the University air. It was not so much that there
were poor scholars—servitors, tabadors and sizars—who
paid for their schooling by menial service instead of
by fee; such a system had always existed and was in a
sense democratic, since it enabled the poorest to receive
the best education the land could offer and kept the
Universities a true mirror of the nation. It was that
new privileges were being accorded to young men of
wealth and rank who did nothing to earn them. It
was seen even in the granting of degrees: " Poor
folks' sons study hard and with much ado obtain
their degrees in Arts and a fellowship," wrote the
indignant Anthony Wood in 1671; " but now noble-

* " Your nephew is likely to keep in good health if he continues to rise
at six o'clock in the morning, which he does not fail of as yet."—Thos.
Dixon of Queen's College to Sir D. Fleming, 20 Aug. 1679, *H.M.C.
Fleming*, 161.

" Dear George. I am very glad you have your health. Rise early, viz.
out at 5 o'clock mornings and go to bed at nine at night, and it will con-
tinue."—Peter Shakerley to George Shakerley at Brasenose College,
Oxford, *Shakerley MSS.*

men's sons are created *Artium Magistri* for nothing, get fellowships and canonries for nothing, and deprive others more deserving of their bread."

It would have mattered little if only the elder sons of noblemen had been treated as a class apart. The nobility was a small class, and comparatively few of its members penetrated to the University. But during the first decade of Charles II's reign, by granting the right to " Gentlemen Commoners " to wear the distinctive badge of silken cap and silver button and expressly denying it to ordinary Bachelors and undergraduates, Oxford established a large new caste and one which in due course was to monopolise the Universities to the exclusion of all others. Time swallowed up alike the " nobleman " with his coloured gown and gold hat-band and the humble servitor labouring by the sweat of his body to earn the noblest reward man can obtain. Yet when it had done so it left only the barren spectacle of Universities that were no Universities since they became closed to all but the sons of gentlemen who could pay their high fees.

In the seventeenth century this evil was only in its infancy. Unearned privilege was resented by many on whom it was conferred: Lord North's son at Cambridge gazed with envy on the poorer scholars from whose company and rough, free pastimes he was debarred, and the head of an Oxford college wrote to a north-country magnate of his sons " that to exempt them from any beneficial exercises is not a privilege but indeed an injury and a loss to them, seeing it is really a depriving them of the just means of attaining learning, which is the end we and they should aim at."[17]

It was an end on the whole achieved. For the country gentlemen of England in the latter seventeenth century formed a real aristocracy, in that they possessed an instinctive preference for the best. By their leadership they elevated the whole nation. They were virile, for they loved manly sports, were ready to undergo pain and knew how to mix with their fellow-men. But they were also cultured. They built commodious and classical houses for themselves and their posterity, filled them with treasures of art, encompassed them with walled gardens to catch the sunlight, made fountains, parterres and grottoes, and planted walks of beech and sycamore. Even a poor Catholic squire, half-ruined by decimations for loyalty to his religion and his king, could not resist the ruling passion of his age and class and overspent his slender income in making new out-buildings, the last, he hoped, which he or his heirs would have to build for many generations to come.

Such men were the patrons of literature and learning. Their libraries show the kind of books they affected, bound in the seemly russet and gold of their age. Theology and the classics came first; among the pur-chases of Sir Daniel Fleming, a typical country gentle-man of his day, are such works as Dr. Taylor's *Dissuasion Against Popery*, Bishop Sanderson's *Five Cases of*

Conscience, and Stillingfleet's *Origines Sacras*. But history, science, and English literature had also an honoured place, and with them came down in the wagon from London Heath's *Chronicle*, Dugdale's *St. Paul's*, Sprat's *History of the Royal Society*, Evelyn's *Sylva* and the Duchess of Newcastle's *Life* of her husband. And when Anthony Wood sent John Cartwright of Aynho his great antiquarian work, handsomely bound and valued by the author at thirty-three shillings, the squire sent him by return fifty shillings " for a requital."[18]

CHAPTER IV

RELIGIO MEDICI

FOR one without faith, it is difficult to understand seventeenth-century England. For faith was part of the air the men of that day breathed. We live in an age when the needs of the body are placed before those of the soul; our gods are the material gods of luxury for the rich and comfort for the poor, and our religious controversies are waged between the adherents of these deities. The God of the seventeenth century was the living God of the Spirit—ever-present, ever-seeing, wonderful beyond all belief to love and terrible to offend. Men dwelt on the thought of Him as they only dwell to-day on the thought of an adored mistress— as a mystery beyond human comprehension, to be worshipped in inexpressible ecstasy and to lose the hope of whom was to lose more than life.

It was this which gave the men of that age their courage and their content. They were afraid—but they were afraid only of a divine mystery. They did not fear, as we do, poverty, discomfort, pain and death. They disliked these evils, but when they came they accepted them as marks of God's intention to be borne with courage and good cheer. "If you be taken away by this dreadful pestilence," wrote one friend to another during the Plague of 1665, " you have had a fair warning and a very long time to prepare yourselves for Heaven. But if God be pleased to favour you with a longer life, the memory of this dismal time will be an antidote for your future against all temptations to sin. It seems to me that every day at London is now (as it were) a Day of Judgment and that all our thoughts are placed on death, on Hell, on Heaven and upon eternity." So viewed, the pestilence was a blessing to arouse men from sleep before it was too late. For the rest he added, " Thy will be done on earth as it is in Heaven is the balsam that cureth all."[1]

Such faith supported our forefathers in every crisis of life, nerved them to bear pain worse than modern medical science permits most of us to know, and buoyed them in the frequent hour of deprivation which the heavy mortality of the day made their lot. " If I do die," wrote Nicholas Culpeper, " I do but go out of a miserable world to receive a crown of immortality." There seemed nothing overstrained or unnatural in such a view of death; dying was the supreme moment of mortal existence—the hour at which a man reaped all that he had sowed.

For the more ordinary occasions of life there sprang from this a natural and homely piety. It strayed into the most casual phrases, sometimes a little strangely. " I got home," wrote a country parson in his diary,

" and found my wife pretty hearty, having taken
physic this day and it working very easily with her: a
great mercy." Divine lessons, it seemed, were hidden
like jewels in every happening. [2]

The national religion as re-established by law in 1660
was Anglicanism—that temperate and rather homely
blend of ancient Catholic ritual and Church government with Protestant tenet which expressed the English
genius for compromise. It was admirably attuned to
attitude of mind of the governing class. During the
Interregnum the Anglican Church had suffered severely
—its priests expelled, estates alienated, and cathedrals
desecrated. With the Restoration it entered upon a
golden period. Its parsons, in their black gowns, square
hats, and vast white bands, enjoyed a revenue of at
least half a million. And in the cathedral towns com-
fortable and dignified colonies of the higher clergy
made themselves as much at home in the world where
rust corrupts and thieves break in as the rooks in the
elms above the prebendal houses they inhabited. At
Wells alone there dwelt under the shadow of the
cathedral no less than seven and twenty prebends and
nineteen canons, besides a Dean, a Preceptor, a Chancellor and an Archdeacon. Here, too, in the cathedral
towns the high pomps of Anglicanism—for a generation
banished as idolatry—were revived in all their glory.
At Exeter the Bishop sat beneath a crimson canopy in
a seat covered with red cloth. It almost seemed to
Catholic observers as though they were in the presence

of their own ancient rites: only there was a difference. For as one of them observed, " under the tabernacle, on a level with the floor of the church, in an enclosure of wood, stood the wife of the Bishop and his children, no less than nine in number." " I have seen," wrote another witness, " the Bishop and the Bishopess, the little Bishops and the little Bishopesses." In England the Apostolic succession appeared to have entered upon an hereditary phase.[3]

Yet throughout the country as a whole, Protestantism held sway in the hearts of the people. In the parish churches neither vestments nor images could hope to find a place: the royal arms, the tables of the Deca-logue and the sepulchral monuments of the landed aristocracy were the only idols permitted. Here the *pièce de résistance* was neither solemn chanting nor liturgy, but the Protestant eloquence of the clergy, whose sermons were alike the favourite listening and reading of our forebears. Two sermons a day on Sundays was the usual fare for all, and an hour a piece was not thought too long. The women-folk were particularly attentive. Some of the more intelligent were in the habit of making shorthand abridgements of the sermon that they might the better afterwards employ their talents in religious controversy. And many a carrier's cart as it lumbered into the heavy shires bore a folio of good Dr. Sanderson's or Dr. Cosin's sermons for the delectation of some country lady. " The Bishop this week," wrote the London correspondent of one such, " comes down to you in the wagon, and I hope brings his blessing with him."[4]

Deep down, and particularly in the towns and in the rich eastern and south-western counties, Puritanism had taken root. After the Restoration it was christened by new names—Fanaticism by its Anglican opponents, Nonconformity by the State. For the rules and ritual of the established Church proved too narrow for acceptance by those who had given themselves to the furious, though diverse, beliefs of Puritan revelation. To foreigners these presented a bewildering variety. There were Anabaptists who believed in the extinction of rank; Libertines who held that sin was only an opinion; Adamites at whose weddings bride and bridegroom wore only a girdle of leaves; Brownists who regarded church bells as popish inventions and broke into prophecy after sermons, and Sabbatarians who believed that divine revelation had been exclusively vouchsafed to Robert Dogs, the London coal-man. " The common people," observed an astonished foreigner, " enjoy a liberty which is incredible, every man following that religion and those rites which most suit his fancy." Yet the followers of all these varied creeds had two things in common: all loathed the Church of Rome and all believed implicitly that they alone were in the right.[5]

Most powerful of the Nonconformist sects were the Presbyterians, whose quarrel with Anglicanism centred round the question of Church government. At the

Restoration it was hoped that they might be induced to conform to a creed which in its essential beliefs differed little from their own, but their dislike of bishops proved too strong. In 1662 over a thousand clergy laid down their livings rather than conform to episcopal government and read the Liturgy. Setting up as private teachers, they did rather better for themselves than had the Anglican clergy whom they had dispossessed during the Interregnum, for their congregations were composed largely of the thriving middle class of the commercial towns, who were ready to pay handsomely for their oratory. In London, Mr. Cotton in the Great Almony, Baxter in Great Russell Street, and the famous Manton in Covent Garden, preached to packed and fashionable congregations every Sunday.

The unlicensed preachers were a great thorn in the side of the Government, whose practices they constantly and quite naturally vilified in their sermons. It seemed to loyal subjects as though they were for ever planning a new revolution and a second republic. But, to do them justice, they were probably quite unconscious of any ulterior purpose but a divine one; their gloomy and awful prognostications on the fate of Church and State seemed in their own eyes as inspired and disinterested as the prophesying of Balaam. " I preached," recorded honest Oliver Heywood, " to a pretty full congregation at the house of Jeffrey Beck; the Lord made it a refreshing night to many souls, though our adversaries watched and gnashed their teeth when they saw so many coming together. I had great liberty of speech in preaching and praying, though," he added a little sadly, "not such melting of heart as sometimes I have enjoyed."[6]

Yet the pride and narrowness that sometimes showed itself in the Puritan leaders was redeemed by the humility and seemly lives of their best followers. Readers of the *Pilgrim's Progress* will remember the song the shepherd boy sang in the Valley of Humiliation. Less familiar is the description of the boatswain, Small, in John Sheffield, Duke of Buckingham's *Memoirs*. Small had been captured with the rest of the crew of the *Royal Katherine* at the battle of Southwold Bay, and, after the captain and officers had been sent off, had been stowed under hatches with the remaining survivors. Unarmed and urging them on with his whistle, he led them in a surprise assault on the Dutch guard and almost miraculously recaptured the ship. " He was a Nonconformist," added Sheffield, " always sober, meek and quiet (even too mild for that bustling sort of employment) and very often gave me an image of those enthusiastic people who did such brave things in our late Civil War; for he seemed rather a shepherd than a soldier and was a kind of hero in the shape of a saint."[7]

Two Christian creeds were outside the pale of English public opinion—Quakerism and Roman Catholicism. The Quakers had few friends. Despite the ultimate gentleness of their tenets, it was not altogether surprising, for their deliberate outrages against contemporary manners won them enemies in all places. One of them made a practice of visiting market-places and rich men's houses, stark naked and smeared with excrement, informing all and sundry that the Lord God would besmear their religion as he was besmeared. Rather naturally the poor man was subjected to " many grievous whippings with long coach whips, stonings and diverse imprisonments." Such excesses, though perhaps not typical, were universally attributed to the Quakers. Until their sturdy integrity of life and constancy of purpose had won them the honoured place they in due course took in the national life, they suffered unceasing persecution.[8]

The Catholics, or Papists as they were called, were universally loathed. They were suspected, quite erroneously, of perpetual machinations against the Government and people of England, who since the days of the Gunpowder Plot had been haunted by a nightmare of red cardinals, black friars, racks, fires and midnight slaughters, and of all the devilries of an alien Church against which their forefathers had rebelled and which ever—so they had been taught from the cradle—plotted to enslave them. Among the upper and middle Protestant classes no reading was more popular than that which exposed (usually at devastating length and with no mincing words) the fallacies of Rome. As for the common people, any demagogue who was unscrupulous enough to play on their anti-Catholic feelings could loose a murderous wild beast. Once a year the London mob processed through the city with effigies of Pope, cardinals and devils stuffed with live cats to make them squeal realistically when burnt, amid shouts of delight, at Smithfield.[9]

From the Catholic point of view, of course, all this bore a very different aspect. The English Catholics were composed almost entirely of members of certain ancient families and their tenantry. These, during the Civil Wars, had shown conspicuous loyalty to the King's cause. After the Restoration they received little reward, for, however much the King might incline to them, he was powerless in face of the universal hatred in which they were held. Fines for " recusancy," which during the " bad times " had sometimes reached as much as twenty pounds a month, were still imposed, though at a milder rate, and priests were forbidden to minister the rites of their religion under pain of death. Even the most common rights of justice were denied to Catholics, who dared not resort to litigation when an unscrupulous opponent could always enforce on them an oath incompatible with their faith or win the case by default. In times of national panic their lot became still more precarious, for then their houses were searched for arms and their liberty restricted by " chains," which forbade them to travel more than a mile or two from their homes. During the " Popish Terror " the best advice a friendly Westmorland justice could give to a Catholic widow was to marry a Protestant who could protect her property and person. Yet persecution only strengthened their constancy. The sons mostly of ancient English Catholic houses, their priests were trained abroad at St. Omer or one of the other English Catholic colleges, and then returned to their own country to pass secretly from house to house, ministering to their flocks in attics and secret oratories, and humbly and faithfully discharging their duty in constant peril of death. Their epitaph has been written by one of their flock, William Blundell of Crosby. " ' We'll hang them,' sayeth a Lancaster Jury. ' We'll crown them,' sayeth Christ." No stronger example of the resilience and strength of faith in the hour of suffering is to be found than in their story.[10]

The crime of intolerance must be set on the reverse of the medal which pictures the grandeur of seventeenth-century religion. It could scarcely be otherwise in an age when an error of dogma was held to imply eternal damnation. Under such circumstances a neighbour of another religion was a greater peril to a man's children than the most dangerous murderer. With intolerance went superstition, though it is arguable that common credulity two hundred and fifty years ago was no greater than it is to-day. To our ancestors the most ordinary natural events were invested with dire meaning: a great gale at Dover seemed, in the eyes of Sir Robert Harley, " a hideous and portending thing; I pray God we may learn the voice of these things." As for comets, these were held to foretell pestilence, fires, frosts, wars, rebellions, and prodigious deaths. Nor was death in its more common forms unheralded. If a bishop was to die at Chichester, a heron appeared and perched on the pinnacle of the cathedral spire. No wonder poor John Burrows, after beholding a coach drawn by six black swine and driven by a negro coachman, assumed that his hour had come and, out of sheer terror, made it so.[11]

Behind all this lay the universal reading of the Bible. Men and women quite uneducated in the literary sense spoke its direct and inspired English; and as their betters did the same, there was a common element in the national tongue such as has existed at no other time. Official jargon had not yet turned the art of administration into an exclusive mystery, though Mr. Pepys in his vast and laborious memoranda was paving a way. An ambassador could still tell in a government dispatch how, when a mob chased its victims seawards, " it pleased Him who bridges the sea with a girdle of sand to put bounds to the fury of the people." And when every sentence rang of the Scriptures men's minds never strayed far from the thoughts of their Maker.

The same reminder was given our fathers by the frequency of death in their midst. Ever-present mortality freed them from the curse of attaching too much importance to their own material achievements and taught them the inevitability of human fate. " For the world," wrote one of their greatest, " I count it not an inn but a hospital, not a place to live in but to die in."

With a high death-rate and the usual practice of child-bearing every year few households were long without funerals. These were celebrated with pomp by an age that loved pageantry for its own sake, and loved it all the more when it signalised the progress of an immortal soul from an imperfect state of proba-tion into a world of infinite glory.* Everything was done to remind men of the dignity of death; most families of consequence possessed at least one enormous mourning bed, completely hung round with black draperies, which perpetually travelled about the country from one bereaved cousin to another. It was the practice for the next of kin to provide as many of the deceased's friends and relations as possible with suits of mourning, rings, gloves and scarves, in addition to distributing largesse among the neighbouring poor in honour of the departed, and to hold a funeral feast of macaroons and biscuits, cold meats and white wine and claret

* " Mrs. Katherine Perceval was very handsomely buried. There were twenty-three poor women in gowns and kerchiefs, after them the maids that watched with her in her sickness, which were some thirty-six, in white gloves and scarves, then John Leyland and the butler in black, after them two doctors of divinity and two bishops; then the corpse, the pall being borne by six knights' daughters, and they led by six knights' sons, who had all white scarves and black cypress over, after them all the ladies and gentlemen, their relations, in mourning, on foot, lead by knights and squires in long black cloaks, and made at least thirty couple, after them the Lord Mayor and Aldermen and other gentlemen and gentlewomen, not in mourning, and then a number of coaches and so to the church, where they were met with the choristers, and afterwards there were at her funeral as many tears as ever I think at one time were shed in that place."—*Hist. MSS. Com. Rep., Egmont Papers*, II. 21.

for the rich, and good store of burnt ale for the poor.[12]

The frequency of funerals followed the state of medical and sanitary knowledge. The speculative generalities of medieval learning still governed medical theory and, though these were not without imaginative truth, they were unrelated to practical observation and experiment. Underlying all was the idea that the movement of everything in the universe was related, and that one had only to understand the divine machinery to discover the elixir of life. So learned men still held that the movements of the stars governed the diseases of the body, that certain days were good for bleeding and others not, that charms and incantations could expel evil influences from the system. There was probably truth in all this, but it was truth whose infinite complexity and detail men had scarcely even begun to trace.

In the medical profession almost universal respect was still paid to the Galenic theory that the body was comprised of liquids or " humours "—two, " blood " and " choler," making for heat and energy, and two, " phlegm " and " melancholy," making for moisture and cold. The proper function of a physician was to preserve the balance between the four, and, in the case of sickness, to reduce whichever had gained an unnatural ascendancy. In pursuit of this theory were the frequent cuppings and bleedings which our ancestors applied to every kind of disease. Often, in days of heavy drinking, such prescription was not inappropriate, but in many cases it was hopelessly at fault. In that of King Charles II, in his last illness, for instance, it was probably responsible for his death. The making of issues to draw out poison from the system was almost as popular. Anthony Wood had one made in his arm in order to recover the hearing of his right ear, and paid five shillings to have it done.[13]

The pseudo-scientific jargon of professional physicians was copied by their clients, the English taking as enthusiastically to amateur doctoring in the seventeenth century as in our own. The learned Elias Ashmole hung three spiders round his neck to drive away the ague, and Ralph Hawtrey wrote to Lady Gawdy how his wife " fell into a violent fit of wind colic mixed with vapours." The latter was a very fashionable disease among ladies, though the travelled Celia Fiennes was of opinion that it was not unconnected with laziness.

Strange and fearful were some of the remedies which our ancestors prescribed. " Take," runs one for a quinsey, " a silk thread dipped in the blood of a mouse, and let the party swallow it down with the pain or swelling in the throat and it will cure him." Another recommends spirit of vitriol for toothache, with a timely caution not to confuse oil with spirit of vitriol, " for if you do it will make foul work." The use of animals for curative purposes was frequently enjoined: cats, fur and all, boiled in olive oil, were said to make an excellent dressing for wounds, while one recipe in a herbal book begins roundly: " Take twenty-four swallows . . ."[14]

Many of the old remedies were based on age-long herb-lore and were often of real value. But in the face of the graver maladies they were helpless. It availed little against the germs of bubonic plague to " take half a handful of rew, likewise of mandragories, featherfew, sorrel burnet, and a quantity of the crops and roots of dragons and wash them clean and seeth them with a soft fire in running water." Smallpox, till vaccination was introduced in the next century, seemed so inevitable that parents sometimes deliberately put their children in the way of taking the infection, so that they might get it over at an age when it was least likely to prove fatal to life or beauty. Infectious disease maintained a constant decimation of the population, which otherwise, with the large families that prevailed, must have increased by leaps and bounds. It was the increase in medical and hygienic knowledge, even more than the improvement in agricultural process and the industrial revolution, that made possible the vast growth of the population in the next century.[15]

The necessary conditions of that growth were being prepared in the reign of Charles II by a little group of brilliant London physicians and surgeons, who, working in the closest contact with the virtuosos of the Royal Society, were beginning to apply deductive and scientific principles to the practice of medicine. Perhaps the greatest of these was Thomas Sydenham. His description of how he discarded the dogmatic theories of his professional brethren in his treatment of a fever to follow nature shows that experimental, truth-loving mind at work:

> "At length I determined, after having bled from the arm, blistered on the nape of the neck, and thrown up, during the first days of the disease, two or three clysters of sugar and milk, to do nothing whatever beyond forbidding the patient meat and fermented liquors. Meanwhile I watched what method Nature might take, with the intention of subduing Nature by treading in her footsteps. Now whilst I so watched the disease, it departed; slowly and safely—still it departed. From thence, therefore, I considered that this method should be applied to all other such cases as I might thenceforward have to treat; a fact of no small magnitude, if we considered either the gravity of the symptom or the uniform success of the treatment."[16]

Even more in the practice of surgery one realises what a burden of pain has been lifted from the back of humanity by the patient industry of the men of science. The best English surgeons of the seventeenth century were probably as skilful and experienced as their modern descendants, but they had to do their work with two supreme disabilities—the absence of chloroform and their ignorance of the nature of septic poisoning. The great surgeon, Thomas Hollier, who cut Pepys for the stone, operated on thirty other patients for the same affliction in the same year and all lived. Shortly afterwards he operated on four more,

Lydia Dwight, stoneware figure, 1674

Here
lyeth y̌ Body
of Richard Winwood Esq̇ one
of y̌ deputy Leiveten̄ants of this
County in the Reigne of King
Charles y̌ second) Son & heir of
y̌ Rt̄ Hbl̄e Sr Ralph Winwood Knt
principle secretary of state to King
James y̌ first. He married Anne
one of y̌ dawghters of Sr Thomas
Head of y̌ County of Barks Knt
And departed this life y̌ 28th
day of Ivne Anno Dom̄i 1688
in y̌ 80th year of his age.
Here lyes also interred y̌ Body
of y̌ said Anne who departed this life
y̌ — day of Mar: Añ Dom̄ 1693

Memorial in Quainton Church to Richard Winwood, d. 1688

who died. The almost certain explanation is that his
instruments became septic. And without chloroform
men and women were called upon to endure prodigies
of suffering, and many died under the shock of an
operation. Evelyn records how during the Third
Dutch War he watched the chirurgeon cut off the leg
of a wounded sailor, "the stout and gallant man
enduring it with incredible patience, without being
bound to his chair as usual on such painful occasions.
I had hardly courage enough to be present," he adds.
In this case courage was unavailing, for, gangrene
ensuing, the second operation cost the poor man his
life.[17]

One aspect of medicine appeared to our ancestors in
a pleasant and even genial guise—the "bath" or
watering-place. More perhaps than any race in the
world the English suffer the periodic instinct to go on
holiday pilgrimage. To-day, with our seaside pleasure-
resorts, our planned tours and ocean cruises, we make
no bones about the matter, but our fathers, perhaps
feeling a little ashamed, hid their childlike desire under
the cloak of some more serious purpose. Chaucer's
Canterbury pilgrims, like hundreds of thousands before
and after, took their summer holiday under the guise
of shrine visiting, but with the Reformation this pretext
was taken away. The Protestant seventeenth century
found its substitute in the pilgrimage of health, to take
the waters, either internally or externally. The fashion
was exploited. All over the country the mineral virtues

of long-neglected waters, that once had gushed and bubbled miraculously to heal good Catholics at the bidding of the local saint, were blazoned abroad by the priests of the new cult of hydropathy. Remote rustic places, like Astrop or Hogshaw, advertised by some enterprising doctor or landowner, found themselves the centre of annual pilgrimages. Lodgings in the adjoining village rose to unheard-of prices, and the precious waters that for generations had been known only to the questing noses of cattle were encircled with stone brims and neat railings.

Especially famous were the waters of Harrogate, " the Yorkshire spa," where the importunate water-women with their sulphur-stained faces—pretty Betty, Kate, and Cousin Doll—would appear at dawn before the beds of gout-plagued old gentlemen, proffering large pots of the healing stuff; Buxton, where lodgings were so scarce that visitors often found themselves sleeping four in a bed; Epsom, where the London merchants from warehouse or Change Alley took their families and occasionally (as in more modern times) the young ladies of other people's; and fashionable Tunbridge Wells, where the Queen went in the mistaken belief that the waters would give the throne an heir.[18]

But greatest of all was Bath. The long, steep descent between rugged, dripping rocks brought the traveller into what once had been a Roman city, but which was now a little seventeenth-century town of jumbled

houses and narrow streets. Here were five famous
baths, of which the largest was the King's, whose
waters rose bubbling hot and tasted " like the water
that boils eggs." In the Cross Bath, the gentlemen sat
on a circular seat surrounding the stone cross in the
centre, while the ladies faced them from arches along
the side, each sitting up to her neck in water with a
laced toilet curtain hanging down from the arch top
to hide the rest of her, and, as though this were not
protection enough, swathed in stiff yellow canvas
garments with episcopal sleeves. These the water
modestly blew out like balloons, " so that your shape is
not seen." Some added to this precautionary attire
cork shoes. And beside each nymph floated a little dish
keeping inviolate from the waters her handkerchief
and nosegay. Above, in the gallery, spectators gazed
and promenaded, while the music played and the
Sergeant of the Bath walked to and fro, complimenting
persons of fashion and showering on them obliging
attentions, for all the world like the chief steward of a
modern cruising liner, and for the same reason. To
add to the decorum of the proceedings, a number of
guides of both sexes stood about in the water, and,
whenever a lady bather wished to move, a female
guide would lend her her arm, while two male guides
at a suitable distance walked before to clear the way.
The departure from the bath was hidden from spectators, but we are more privileged. For we know that
as the lady bather ascended the steps that led out of the

bath her costume dropped from her, slipping back into the sulphurous waters, while, as she still ascended, a flannel night-gown was smartly dropped over her head by her maid, the guides behind twitching down the tail of it. Thus clad, she entered a small chamber called the " Slips," where a fire and a sedan chair awaited her, in which last, completely enclosed in red baize and sweating profusely, she was carried, chair and all, to the bedroom of her lodgings by two chairmen, and put to bed.

This was for the morning; in the afternoon the company took its diversion in the pleasant walks of the King's Mead and the cloisters, or visited the little cake-houses for gossip and the consumption of fruit lulibubs. And in the evening, while the hot, bubbling springs refilled the baths, there were balls.[19]

CHAPTER V

HABIT AND PASTIME

WITHOUT sturdy frames and cheerful spirits our
fathers could scarcely have borne much that
their lot entailed. Strong drink and wholesome food
were necessities. Of the former they drank more than
we; the regulation allowance of beer for a common
sailor was a gallon a day. Water was often hard to
obtain and still more frequently bad; in important
cities like Worcester and Chester it was carried up
from the river in leather bags slung across the backs
of horses and sold in the streets.[1]

The national drinks were beer and ale. The former
was brewed mainly at home and stored in vast vessels
bound with iron hoops. But there were also many
public brewers, and in 1688 twelve million barrels
were sold to a total population of not much more than
five millions. Ale was often prepared with the aid of
some foreign substance such as a capon, which was
left to grow putrid along with the malt, thus giving
body to the drink. Much depended on the local water
used for the brew; it was held that the farther north
one went the better and stronger the ale, Yorkshire

having the pre-eminence in this respect. Here it was the custom of innkeepers to provide free food for all who bought their liquor.*

In the Western counties cider took the place of ale as the staple drink and was sold in every inn. The best brews had a more than local reputation, particularly those of Worcestershire, where Lord Scudamore of Holme Lacy laid the whole county under his debt by bringing to perfection the famous redstreak cider, which Grand Duke Cosmo on his visit to England christened *Vin de Scudamore*. London vintners were not slow to follow the Duke's hint, and bought up vast quantities of Devonshire cider, which, with the help of Middlesex turnips, they transformed, to their great profit, into very passable claret.[2]

For the gentry great quantities of foreign wine were imported to England from France, Spain, the Atlantic islands, the Rhineland and Italy. Even Hungarian wine was occasionally bought by connoisseurs of an experimental turn. Many country gentlemen did their own purchasing direct from abroad, subsequently bottling from hogshead or runlet in their own cellars. Vintage wines were still unknown, and the whole business

* The more famous brews, such as Northdown ale from Deal, were bottled and sold in the better taverns. Fancy varieties were also much sought after—such was mum, which was brewed with wheat instead of hops; buttered ale, which was warmed and flavoured with sugar, cinnamon and butter; and lamb's wool, which was mixed with the pulp of apples. Other popular made-up drinks were metheglin, a mead made of fermented honey; hypocras, a mixture of red wine sugared and spiced; and syllabub, which was deliciously but indigestibly comprised of sweetened wine and cream.

was apt to be somewhat of a gamble. Yet a body
of good taste was already in process of formation,
which in time was to turn the making of wine into a
fine art. Those—and there were many in the England
of Charles II—who had known exile in France and had
there grown used to the produce of the great vineyards,
were no longer content with the heavy English brews.
" When you are resolved to enjoy yourself," wrote
one such to a friend in France, " and the pretty maid of
your house brings out that lovely bottle of sparkling
wine, remember—oh! remember the misery that
muddy ale hath brought upon mortal man." Attempts
were even made to grow vines out of doors in England:
Mr. Howard's vine at Deardens, near Dorking, under
the wooded shelter of the North Downs, was said to
produce excellent wines. And over the stone porch
of my former home in Buckinghamshire is still a vine,
planted by Edmund Verney in the sixteen-sixties, which
bears each year a crop of tiny green grapes.[3]

After the Restoration a new vice (or so it seemed to
superior persons) sprang up among the commonalty of
England, that of substituting brandy for the national
beverage. The habit was said to have spread during
the Dutch Wars from the sailors of the Dutch marine
to those of the English. One result was an increase of
drunkenness in the seaports, the potency of " strong
waters " proving rather too much for a people already
accustomed to consume a very liberal quantity of liquor.
Sobriety was not an English virtue. The cultured and

temperate Roger North describes how, entertaining the Mayor and Aldermen of Banbury at his brother's house, Wroxton, he so plied them—sitting, standing and walking—that they spent the night in ditches homeward bound, while he himself retired "like a wounded deer to a shady, moist place," and there lay down and "evaporated four or five hours." At Liverpool, even under the Puritan régime in 1657, a sober and devout man like William Blundell could subscribe a letter: "And so in as good a case as this drunken town will permit at four in the afternoon." And when the great Admiral Tromp, as deadly with a bottle as a cannon ball, visited England, he met his match—and it was our senior University that had the honour. For Dr. Speed, with five or six more as able as himself at wine or brandy, got him to the "Crown Tavern," and there so filled him with both that at twelve at night he was carried unconscious to his bed.[4]

Drinking so much, our ancestors usually ate fewer meals than we. Their chief meal, dinner, took place at any time between twelve and half past one. Breakfast, in the modern sense, they did not eat, but, as the contemporary name of "morning draught" implies, drank. It was taken, if taken at all, at any time between dawn and eleven in the morning, and usually consisted of ale or a cup of wine, or in winter of purl (which was beer warmed and flavoured with herbs) or mulled claret. To savour the draught pickled oysters, radishes or anchovies were sometimes eaten: on grander occasions a neat's tongue, a collar of brawn or even a cold game-pie. Occasional variants were a pot of chocolate for settling the stomach after a debauch, or a cup of whey, which the lawyers, as they came into West-minster Hall of a morning, much affected. Tea and coffee were not yet breakfast drinks: these were only just making their appearance from China and Turkey, and were taken at special tea- and coffee-houses as a rather solemn ritual. The former was sometimes known as China ale. During the reign the habit for both developed rapidly.

The English of that age were great meat-eaters. Two pounds of best salted beef was the daily allowance of a common seaman. Reformers pointed out that such a diet accounted for the calentures, scarbots and skin diseases from which the islanders suffered and recommended to them the lighter fare of their neigh-bours. They were little heeded. For the rest, the dishes of our forebears were more mixed and diverse than ours; the food of Germany at the present day is per-haps the best parallel. Like the modern Germans, they particularly loved anything with a relish, a taste catered for in their preserved foods—a glass of gherkins, a barrel of scallops or a neat's tongue. Their cheese too they liked strong: Stilton, " the Parmesan of England," was brought to the table with a special spoon for scoop-ing up the maggots.[5]

But most food was eaten fresh, for the science of preserving was still in its infancy. Owing to the badness of transport, it was difficult to find a market for surplus fresh food, which thus tended to be remarkably cheap in the locality which produced it. This made travelling in England a great delight for the gourmet. On the Dart one could buy fresh lobsters at a few pence apiece, and in South Wales, Milford Haven oysters at sixpence a hundred. Special local foods were to be had everywhere. In Lancashire, where oats were universally grown, oat cakes or "clasp bread," as big as pancakes were laid upon the table in baskets and eaten with butter, black cheese and strong ale, the staple diet of the north.

Of fresh, wholesome ingredients for food there was no lack. The population was still small and agriculture flourished, with varied crops and plenty of home-reared mutton and beef, milk and poultry. Compared with those of other countries, the English common people fed magnificently. Game, moreover, was plentiful in the forests, heaths and marshes which still covered a great part of the country.[6]

Being so well provided with materials, the housewives and cooks of the day could afford to be lavish, and were: the humblest country-house recipe-book would cheerfully recommend the making of a dish with a grandiloquent "Take two quarts of cream and the yolks of ten eggs." For here was God's plenty. And after their kind our ancestors were splendid cooks, every mother handing down to her daughter the mysteries of that science on which more than any other

the material well-being of mankind depends. Their
humblest recipes were princely:

> "Cut a shoulder of mutton like a shoulder of venison,
> take samphire, parsley, a little onion, a little green shallott,
> an anchovy, a few capers, then peel a very little nutmeg,
> salt, pepper, shred with beef suet, as small as can be: so
> stuff it outside and inside and place it upon the spit. Pour
> into your pail some samphire liquor with a spoon; when it
> begins to dry baste it with butter and lard; about a quarter of
> an hour before it is roasted take an onion sliced in half . . .
> take up the meat and hold it over the dish and slab it so
> that the gravy may run into it. Squeeze an orange into it.
> . . . The samphire and parsley must be twice as much as
> the other things. It will make good roasting."[7]

Compared with our more monotonous regimen, their
ordinary meals had a curiously haphazard quality.
There was about them the uncertainty of a picnic;
one never quite knew when one would dine or on
what. One day Pepys came home to dine on three
eels that his wife had just bought from a street hawker,
on another on some roast beef from the cook-shop
near by, on a third on a dish of " pease porridge and
nothing else." When he went out to dine with his
father, he was unlucky, for the household was busy and
there was nothing but a small dish of powdered beef
and a dish of carrots; on another occasion he and a
friend tried three cook-shops on their way from Westminster to London, but could get no dinner at any of
them, till at a fourth, near Temple Bar, they lighted
on a pullet ready roasted.

But in the preparation of their feasts display, variety and above all quantity of dishes were demanded. Humble folk of the middle rank, such as Pepys at the time when he first began his diary, would entertain five or six friends on a dish of marrow-bones, a leg of mutton, a loin of veal, a plate of pullets and larks, a great tart, a neat's tongue, a dish of anchovies, another of prawns and cheese, all placed on the table at once. These were set off against as much plate or fine pewter as could be mustered on side-table or dresser. The meal began about one and continued for several hours, being followed by cards, games, music and the drinking of wine (and later in the reign sometimes of tea) till seven or eight at night. For most people, of course, such feasts were not a very frequent luxury.

Among the nobility the conventions of the table were still more elaborate. For the first course there stood before every trencher on the table " a sallet, a fricassee, a boiled meat, a roast meat, a baked meat and a carbonado." Salads were of four kinds, green, boiled, grand and compound, stewed fresh-water fish being served with the roast meats and sea-fish with the baked. A second course followed of every kind of fowl from mallard, teal and snipe to peacock and quail, with baked pies and tarts of marrow-bone and quinces —marzipans, comfits, preserves and fruits. Sometimes there was a third course of choice sweetmeats. All these were spread about the table in circular dishes, great and small, till scarcely an inch of the tablecloth was uncovered. The more dishes, the greater the dignity of the host; at a small dinner of sixteen guests at Dublin Castle in 1666, the Duke and Duchess of Ormonde provided seventeen dishes for the first, seventeen for the second, and thirteen for the third course.

The great, who kept open house for numerous retainers and guests, dined at long tables covered with white cloth and surrounded by tapestried stools: chairs with arms were still rare and were provided only for very important persons. In the highest circles of all (but nowhere else) a single knife and fork, " tastefully arranged," were set at each place. Guests were expected, however, to bring their own spoons. Here and there, wedged between the army of dishes were large silver monteiths of water with notched brims, from which glasses were hung to cool; these, however, only came into general use towards the end of the reign.[8]

Both during and after the feast drink circulated freely. It was considered bad form for a gentleman to sip his wine; rather, keeping his eyes devoutly on the bottom of his glass, he was expected to drain it in a single draught. This and the drinking of toasts kept the rate of consumption generously high. Toast-making was attended by an elaborate ritual. When for this purpose a guest addressed himself to his neighbour, the latter removed his hat (which etiquette otherwise demanded should be worn at the table) and inclined his head towards him. " Bow to him that drank to you, and then apply yourself to him whose lady's health is drunk, and then to the person that you drink to," is Pepys's description of the new fashion of giving toasts. Sometimes the host would walk the length of the table pledging each guest in turn, and generally before the meal began the King's health was drunk standing, with a salvo of cheers.[9]

To such highly civilized persons as the French, much of this English magnificence seemed a little lacking in neatness and gentility. There were no bisks and pottages so dear to the French heart; there were too many ill-warmed dishes, the pastry was coarse and badly baked, and the stewed fruits and confectionery were often uneatable. There was probably truth in this, for then as now the English were happier in their familiar and domestic occasions than in grander entertainments. Foreigners were pained also by the absence of ewers, a single large basin, into which all alike dipped fingers and napkins, sufficing at all but the grandest feasts. There was also a distressing scarcity of forks, which were only very slowly making their way on to the English dinner-table. And even when they were induced to use these instruments our countrymen seemed to be at a loss what to do with them, since they had to be cautioned not to plunge them at every mouthful into the common dishes and not to pick their teeth with them.

Indeed, polite foreigners found it necessary to tell the English a great deal about their table-manners. A little work called *Rules of Civility* was translated from the French towards the end of the reign, and by what they were warned not to do we can see all too plainly what our forefathers did. Bones were broken on the table and gnawed and vast pieces of meat thrust into the mouth by hand or knife. "You must not," this polite mentor urges, "blow your nose publicly at the table, or, without holding your hat or napkin before your face, wipe off the sweat from your face with your handkerchief; to claw your head, to belch, hawk and tear anything up from the bottom of your stomach," it continues, "are things so intolerably sordid that they are sufficient to make a man vomit to behold them." It appears that the generality of the English were not aware of this.[10]

This new "civility" was a force to be reckoned with in Restoration England, though at first it only affected the Court and the more fashionable of the gentry. It came from France, where young Louis— "the sun King"—was inaugurating that wonderful era in every form of art which bears his name. Into England flowed after 1660 an ever-increasing stream of French ideas and modes of life. Fine Gallic gentlemen surprised simple Englishmen with their quaint airs and graces; French *modistes* appeared with fans and petticoats and "the fashones" to tempt the purse and adorn the persons of our English ladies. Everything new came from Paris, the Mecca of the civilised world, from sedan-chairs and dainty silver brushes for cleaning the teeth to Chatelin's famous fricassees and ragouts.[11]

In the polite world of the capital and the great provincial capitals, York, Exeter, Chester, Norwich and Shrewsbury, " civility " came to regulate every human relationship. An elaborate etiquette arose to govern the modes of address and friendship, in which all was strictly based on rank and precedence. If, for instance, we are told in the *Rules of Civility*, " you meet with a person of quality in the streets, you must run presently towards the channel or post yourself so that he may pass by with his left hand towards you and his right hand free, and the same rule is to be observed with coaches." Still harder was the case of a private gentleman walking between two lords: whenever they reached the end of the street he must remember to turn towards the greater of the two, while if they happened to be of equal rank, he must turn first towards one and then the other. It made life rather complicated for the initiated, but (and this was a consolation) left no chance for the uninitiated to compete.

There was no limit to the deference due to a lord. " If," we are told, " his Lordship chances to sneeze, you are not to bawl out ' God bless you, Sir,' but, pulling off your hat, bow to him handsomely, and make that observation to yourself." Not merely were his acquaintances to refrain in their conversational fervour from pulling him by the buttons or punching him in the stomach—" for that would be saucy "—but

The royal gardener, John Rose, presents the first pineapple grown in England to Charles II

A Wiltshire scene, c. 1675

they were constantly by their attitude to make him and all the rest of the world aware of the profound respect in which they held him. If his servant brought one of them a message, he must rise to receive it, and some, we are told, " have been so refined in foreign parts that they will neither be covered nor sit with their backs turned towards the picture of an eminent person." Friends who called on a peer were warned not to give more than one knock; if it was unanswered the only remedy left was to scratch gently and respectfully on the door. And if while they sat with his Lordship they had occasion to spit, they were urged to do it with an obsequious air, sideways, and into the fire. Even in church they were compelled to maintain the same ceremony; indeed, here, as the author of the *Rules of Civility* justly observes, a man's natural reverence in kneeling must be increased by " seeing so many persons of Quality in the same posture."[12]

All this decorum tended to make high society a little tedious. If one was entertaining, a whole regiment of rules governed the place and manner of receiving guests and bidding them farewell: at which point in hall or on stairs one was to meet them, how far in bowing to incline the head towards them, where to bid them be seated, and when to sit oneself. When the Grand Duke Cosmo of Florence had feasted Charles II, after the passage of many formal expressions of courtesy and gratitude, the Duke accompanied His Majesty out to his carriage, where the King (doubtless sincerely, for his host was a profound bore), " entreated the prince to retire to rest as soon as possible." But the Duke was determined to outdo the King in civility, and, keeping his hand in the open carriage door, dexterously slipped into it just as it started, and, in spite of vigorous royal opposition, remained in it till it reached Whitehall. And it took a Duke and the first Minister of the Crown to get the triumphant Cosmo back to his own lodgings with the proper degree of respect due to his rank.[13]

In other respects the new etiquette was the outward sign of a more social and civilised attitude of mind. Old-fashioned Anthony Wood angrily recorded in 1675 that since the King was restored it was looked upon as a piece of pedantry to introduce Latin tags into one's discourse, to dispute theology at table or indeed to be earnest or zealous in anything. But, though the old England that had done so may have been a very devout place, it had not been an easy one to live in. In this King Charles II was a creator. In a quarter of a century he did something to transform his rough realm into a gentler and more urbane mould. His conception of a gentleman was the model by which the chivalry of England now learned to dress itself; it was, as he put it in a nutshell, " to be easy oneself and to make everybody else so." It was a conception not unneeded, for in neither of these respects did the English excel in the years before the Restoration.[14]

The old manner of England was rough, unreasoning,

and boisterous. Fighting was the darling pastime of its people. In Moorfields, on holidays, the butchers, out of hereditary hatred, fell upon the weavers till they were glad to pull off their aprons and hide them in their breeches; or sometimes it would be the weavers who won, wounding and bruising all their rivals and calling out round the town: " A hundred pounds for a butcher! " Since there were no police, the warlike tastes of the people were quite untrammelled. The very Inns of Court were riotous, and when the Lord Mayor elected to go to dinner in the Temple with his sword borne before him, the students pulled it down and besieged him all day in a councillor's room. Even in Oxford a learned antiquary belaboured one of his fellow-dons whenever he met him, giving him many a bloody nose and black eye.[15]

Among the lesser gentry of a people so turbulent duels were almost incessant. Two strangers at night, jostling for the wall about the New Exchange, whipped out their swords and killed each other on the spot. Honest John Reresby, lord of many hundred acres, related with pride how, dining at a neighbour's house, he quarrelled with a young gentleman engaged to his host's daughter and all but spoilt the match: " We should have fought the next day, but considering better of it he submitted—though it was he who received the affront, for I threw a glass of wine in his face." The King was always trying in vain to moderate this passion in his people.[16]

This pugnacity the English carried into the concerns of State, which, after twenty years of wont, they regarded as peculiarly their own. In this they astonished foreigners; a Frenchman reported that the very boatmen wanted the milords to talk to them about State affairs while they rowed them to Parliament. With those who disagreed with their views they had a short and ready way. When the French ambassador omitted to light a bonfire at his door to celebrate an English victory over the Dutch the mob smashed his windows and all but grilled him on his own furniture. His successor, after describing an attempt to kill the first Minister of the Crown in his own bedroom, could only comment: " When I reflect that this land produces neither wolves nor venomous beasts, I am not surprised. The inhabitants are far more wicked and dangerous."[17]

A vent for all this animal energy and excess of spirits was provided by the national passion for exercise and field sports. Game was plentiful and, though the game laws were already beginning to set limits to it, its pursuit still provided recreation for a large proportion of the country population. Hedge squires and yeomen with a few hundred acres would keep hounds and hunt hares over their own land and the neighbouring commons. The very judges on circuit would take a day off for the chase, and even the London shopkeepers had their common hunt in Epping Forest, with the Lord Mayor as master.

Deer were hunted by the larger landowners in the forests and great parks. In the glades of the woods beneath the South Downs the red deer still grazed, and sometimes delicate stepping creatures from Epping, Enfield or Windsor were seen in the suburbs of London. The King himself loved to be up by five to hunt the stag in the forests round the metropolis, where he would tire out all the horses and come home in muddy velvet cap and hunting-jacket with scarcely an attendant beside him. Fox-hunting was still in its infancy, for the large packs of to-day were unknown, and hounds were free to follow every scent with the whole neighbourhood running and shouting after the field.* But the most universal sport was hare-hunting. Beagles and greyhounds were bred everywhere, and the accounts of any country estate abound with entries of sheep's feet and livers bought for their consumption. " Your Wrench," writes one squire to another, " is now one of the very best greyhounds in the county, hedges well and tops better and bears pretty well." Here were the real passions of the gentry from the cradle to the grave.[18]

It was a wholesome regimen, and one that gave the

---

* Though sometimes a fox, encountered by chance, would give a splendid run, as witness the following: " I was a fox-hunting yesterday with my Lord Lexington in Windsor Forest. We found a fox, ran him about six miles, earthed him, dug him out, set him down in the middle of the Forest; he ran two hours and a half afterwards, returned to the place where we found him, and scratched into too strong an earth. In all we ran him nearly 25 miles. This," the writer adds, " is the only fox chase I have seen this three years."—Robt. Jennings to Thos. Coke, 23 Nov. 1669, H.M.C. Cowper, II, 394.

nation a long line of bluff, cheerful, healthy rulers—
men such as the first Lord Shaftesbury's friend, Squire
Hastings of Woodlands in Dorset. Long, thin, fiery-
haired, in aged clothes of green which even when new
had never cost more than five pounds, he kept all
manner of hounds that ran—buck, fox, hare, otter and
badger—and his house was full of hawks, hounds and
terriers. His walls were hung with gamekeepers' poles
and the skins of foxes and marten cats, and the floor of
his hall was strewn with marrow-bones. "He was
well natured, but soon angry, calling his servants
bastards and cuckoldry knaves, in which he often
spoke truth to his own knowledge, and sometimes in
both, though of the same man. He lived to be an
hundred and never lost his eye-sight, but always wrote
and read without spectacles and got on horseback
without help. Until past fourscore he rode to the death
of a stag as well as any."

With the improvement of firearms and the enclosures of large tracts of hitherto open country,
shooting was taking the place of the older sports of
hawking and fowling, though the former was still
followed with short-winged hawks on heath and down-
land. King Charles, in his latter years, loved to canter
after his hawks with his red-coated falconers about
him across the Winchester hills. For the fowler, load-
ing was still a slow and laborious business. Therefore
the *Gentlemen's Recreation* recommended "in using
this weapon you should shoot not at a single fowl if

you can compass more within your level; and, if on a tree, hedge or the ground, seek the convenientest shelter you can of hedge, bank, tree or the like to be absconded from the fowl seeing you, which is very offensive to them, and being within shot and a fair mark, lose no time but let fly." But an enterprising Gloucestershire squire, Sir William Kyte of Ebrington, had a double-barrelled gun made for him for bringing down the seamews as they winged their way in flights over the Cotswolds. And though only foreign potentates like the French King knew the organised delights of great battues,* English gentlemen were everywhere training pointers, setters, and retrievers, while one north-country squire was in the habit of using detachments of colliers from his mines to beat woodcock.[19]

Horse-racing, which had grown up through the centuries out of the commercial needs of horse-dealers, was given a new status by the enthusiastic patronage of King Charles II. Nine years after the Restoration he paid his first visit to Newmarket, where his father and grandfather had occasionally attended horse-races. Henceforward he returned to the little town for a few weeks every spring and autumn. Here he was at his happiest. " The King is highly pleased," wrote one of his attendants, " with all his Newmarket recreations;

---

* " With Lord Brouncker to Sir Robert Long, whom we found in his closet and among other things he told us of the plenty of partridges in France, where he says the King of France and his company killed with their guns in the plain de Versailles 300 and odd partridges at one bout."
—*Pepys, Diary*, 21 March, 1666.

by candlelight yesterday morning and this morning hunting the hare; this afternoon he hawks and courses with greyhounds. . . . As thou prizest earthly felicity bring a Maid of Honour behind thee." Such felicity was seldom wanting. Under the genial patronage of this prince, himself no mean horseman or judge of horseflesh, the first of English sports found a fitting home. Charles loved the informality of the place, the fleet running of the delicate-shaped creatures he imported from the East, the evenings among the jockeys, where he " put off the king." On the great wind-ridden heath, the very centre and epitome of England, he was free.

At Newmarket Charles built himself a house in the long village street opposite the " Maidens " Inn, and established the headquarters of English horse-racing. In his stables Arab horses, fed on beverages of soaked bread and fresh eggs, were tended with all the art imaginable, while, on the heath beyond, the King himself in plain country dress, marked only by the badges of the George and Garter, waited with his cortège on the course, ready to gallop beside the jockeys to the winning-post, where trumpets and drums acclaimed the victor.

The new national sport tended to be fast in more ways than one, as the names of some of the horses show—" Jack-come-tickle-Me, " " Kiss-in-a-Corner," " Sweetest-when-Naked." There was a good deal of gambling attached to it; there is a record of a visiting

French astrologer losing his own and his client's money by wrongly prognosticating three times together which horse would win. Defoe in the next age speculated as to whether this part of the sport had not introduced a " sharp tricking temper " into the gentry of England. Quiet country race-meetings that had hitherto been little noticed attracted great concourses to see the famous horses that racing magnates, like Lord Wharton or Tregonwell Frampton, hawked about the country, and new meetings sprang up everywhere. The old-fashioned bells for which local squires and farmers had competed gave way to fine plates and cups of silver and gilt, and gentlemen backed their horses against one another on Banstead or Burford Downs, Chester Roodee or Quainton Meadow, with elaborate stakes and forfeitures. The great annual event at Quainton—all the rest of the year the quietest of country villages—has been drawn by Edmund Verney, in a letter written on the last day of his life to his brother, the Turkey merchant:

" Understanding from my son what good sport there was at Quainton race the first day where Chesney the horse courser made thousands of men run after him with their swords drawn, I went next day myself to the race and carried my cousin Cary and my daughter in the hopes to meet with the like diversion, but he was not so obliging to the company to give them the same pastime. So my cousin Denton's man, Valentine Budd, rid for the Plate and won it. It was a silver server. His horse that won it was a grey. There was a child rid over and almost killed, and old

Claver of Weedon fell off from his horse, being very drunk."[20]

In quieter and more pastoral mood were the humbler disciples of Izaak Walton, who with tackle and fly took their age-long pleasure (and sometimes colds) in English water-meadows, or the bowlers who congregated on country-house lawns on summer evenings. Bowls was the great summer game of the gentry; even during the Interregnum the gentlemen of Staffordshire and Cheshire competed against each other on Brereton Green. His Majesty himself sometimes condescended to throw a wood with his subjects, as Duke Cosmo beheld him doing in the middle of the race-course at Newmarket in the spring of 1669. More general in its appeal, because more easily played, was ninepins; there was a game to be had in any inn that had a garden, and one could generally get a fellow to set up the pins for a pint of ale. In a quiet way it was possible to win quite a lot of money by backing one's skill at bowls and ninepins.[21]

Though real tennis was already old in fame as the most expensive and exclusive of sports, cricket and football were still village games, with many local variants, and competing with a hundred others. Football was very rough and played usually in frosty weather by large crowds, who filled the streets with flying balls and made life distinctly uncomfortable for passers-by. Trap-ball, tip-cat, baseball and innumerable other games were favoured by different towns and villages, for the people still made their own pastimes locally as they made their food and drink. Then there was cock-fighting, bull-running and bear-baiting, whose professional showmen perpetually perambulated the country; while the big country fairs brought their time-honoured store of performing apes, jugglers, fire-eaters, Dutchmen who stood on weathercocks and girls who walked precariously but alluringly on stilts. [22]

Besides all this every village had its regular feasts and traditional revelries, which all the edicts of Puritanism in high places had not yet been able to extinguish. At the " Yule Plough," when the year began, the sword-dancers in white shirts and ribbons danced across the frozen fields with cracking whips, led by grotesques wearing tails and old women's heads, and before every house that would not give them largesse they ploughed up the soil. In the summer there were the May Day games, when young men and maidens (who did not always return so) went out into the woods long before dawn to pick flowers and branches. At Whitsun there was the Lamb Feast, and on Midsummer Eve wrestling and dancing round the midnight fire in the village street. Every season and event of the agricultural year was celebrated in due form, with mumming plays, hobby-horses, fiddles and bagpipes, and though the music was not always of the best and many of the ancient rites were wearing rather thin, there was still life and zest in it and a common national social tradition. [23]

For winter evenings our ancestors had plenty of indoor games to amuse them. Ancient gentlemen in the country, who liked to do things in the old Elizabethan fashion, were given to backgammon, which they were apt to intimidate more reluctant juniors into playing with them. Tables or dominoes were also fairly popular: there was room for gambling in all this, though some preferred to dice alone over a bottle and Parmesan like Trice in *The Wild Gallant*. But the greatest indoor favourites were cards, which ranged from ombre, the new fashionable game at Court, to homely gleek, and that quiet, respectable game cribbage.[24]

One must picture them at play on a winter evening in some country house, when the men had lit their long pipes and the women sat over their embroidery frames in the withdrawing-room or smaller parlour. The background should be in tapestry—a suit of the Apostles in bright reds, greens and blues, or of Hero and Leander, Vulcan and Venus, or Cæsar's triumphs; and outside in the gallery through the open door a gilt frame and the features of some friend or relation in Mr. Lely's dark colours staring in a little ominously. The room is lit by candles against silver sconces round the walls (the light too is caught by long gilt mirrors), and by the flames of the great wood fire, crowned in its stone heraldic fireplace and sentried by shining andirons. The company—a numerous one, for our forefathers with their vast families loved to crowd together in a house—are seated on turned stools bright with silk and brocade, the master and mistress alone sitting on straight, tall-backed chairs, fantastically carved. The heavy curtains, a striped turkey carpet or two on the floor and tapestry covers for the tables complete the colour of the background, while the firelight plays softly on the dark shades of the furniture— the English oak of the older pieces and the fine ebony, japan, or surinam spicklewood of the newer ones— cabinet, bureau and scriptor. So they sit till the torches come to light them through cold rooms to great beds, curtained deep with valance, hanging and counterpane.

Music and dancing complete the tale of their recreations, but these were the greatest. And the former was made for the latter, for in all the music they composed, even at its most wistful, there was a certain rhythmical insistence which invited listeners to tread a measure. There was a wonderful range in the instruments they used—lute, theorbo and guitar, whose strings were touched with the fingers, cittern and dulcimer, which were sounded with a hammer; the bowed instruments, viol, bass-viol, treble-viol and violin, with which English families delighted to gather for an evening of chamber music; the flutes, flageolet and recorder (which a tired man might take out to while away an hour stolen from business beside the Echo in St. James's Park), and the virginals, spinet, and harpsichord in their delicate-shaped frames, over whose keyboards and black and white notes the hands moved as over a modern piano.* Singing was universal, while every village had its bell-ringers and its string-choir. Larger places had their band of "town music," which travellers might command to attend them at their inn, and which sometimes did so without being commanded. The Cambridge trumpeters came before dawn to the "Bear Inn" to give the travellers a *levite*; Pepys, going down the river, shared a boat with a stranger who, proving a man of music, sang catches with him all the way; on a moonlight night he, with his wife and maids, sang in the garden, with mighty pleasure to themselves and neighbours " by their casements opening." Every substantial family in town and country made its own music as it made its own jam; the men and boys on viol, harpsichord and double bass, the girls with lute, spinet and guitar. In their rough amateur, but very competent, way they excelled in the old English music—" like sitting," as Roger North remembered it, " in a pleasant cool air on a temperate summer evening, when one may think or look or not, and still be pleased."[25]

* But their strings, unlike those of the piano, were plucked, not struck

CHAPTER VI

THE MEANS OF LIFE

DWARFED by that of its neighbour France, with her 19,000,000 inhabitants, and smaller than that of Spain or Austria, the population of England stood at about 5,000,000 at the beginning of Charles II's reign, and probably at 500,000 more at the end. The six northern counties, which together were assessed for purposes of taxation lower than either Sussex or Suffolk, accounted for only a fraction of this figure. Gregory King, the statistician, writing in the years that followed Charles II's death, reckoned that it included 16,600 gentlemen, 10,000 merchants, 10,000 clergy, 10,000 public servants and officials, 9,000 naval and military officers, 15,000 lawyers and 9,000 employed in one or other of the liberal arts. About one-sixth of the total population, or 180,000 families, were yeomen, and 2,500,000 agricultural labourers, most of whom had some small stake, if only a right of common, in the land. Another 1,500,000 were town-dwellers. Of this latter class a third was concentrated in London; the remainder lived in country towns, of which the largest, Bristol and Norwich, had not much more than 30,000 inhabitants.[1]

All these were fed, clothed, and housed by the products of English soil. It was not ungenerous. A temperate climate afforded it the finest pastures for sheep and cattle in the world, its fields produced adequate crops—wheat in the south and coarser oats and barley in the north—and its numerous heaths, fens and forests, covering, it was reckoned, half the kingdom, supported vast quantities of poultry and geese, wild-fowl and swine.

With so great a proportion of the agricultural population yeomen farmers and their families, possessing land by freehold or copyhold tenure, the basis of agriculture was broad and liberal. In addition there were a large number of non-yeomen tenant-farmers, while the peasantry enjoyed substantial rights of grazing and turfage. Unfortunately, the larger gentry, whose ranks were continually reinforced by retired merchants investing their capital in land, were tending to swallow up their smaller neighbours, whose fields they bought whenever the chance offered.[2]

For once the Civil Wars were out of the way the value of land began to rise steadily as a result of agricultural improvements. The pace of these was set by the gentry, whose virility and superior education fitted them to act as pioneers, and whose comparative poverty during and after the years of the Interregnum stimulated them to better husbandry. Everywhere they were busy experimenting with new methods. Their enterprise and daring—for they risked largely—

gave value and utility to land hitherto unproductive. In the barren places of Lancashire a poor hedge-squire like William Blundell of Crosby was laying out £5 an acre for marling, while the Essex squires brought chalk from the barren Kentish cliffs to enrich their own waste lands. Such enterprise was needed, if ever England was to maintain a larger population; for the prevailing system of agriculture, though sound, was ancient and unprogressive; in midland counties, like Oxfordshire and Leicestershire, the ploughs were still wheelless and drawn by oxen.

Where the innovators were successful a rich reward was theirs. In some cases the rentals of lands enclosed increased threefold; those of one Cambridge college rose from £140 to £537 per annum. Farms in the prosperous south-west sold in good times at twenty-eight years' purchase; in the eastern counties at twenty or twenty-one; in the turbulent, barren north, with its peel-towers, moss-troopers, and parish bloodhounds, at only sixteen. The average rent for good arable land was about 5s. or 6s. an acre; for pasture-land perhaps 3s. more. Lord Arlington let his farms in Sussex at 6s. an acre, payable half-yearly, giving his tenants full liberty to use land for plough or pasture, or sublet it as they chose; less enlightened landlords were inclined to oppress their tenants with restrictive covenants. But rack-renting was seldom employed; with the constant difficulty of finding good tenants it did not pay, the squire who opened his mouth too wide being soon left with nothing but men of straw for tenants, or with his farms thrown useless on his hands.* As ever in England, it paid to be reasonable.[3]

Tithes were already becoming a burden. A Cheshire farmer in 1658 was paying 5s. an acre on wheat, 2s. 4d. on oats, and 3s. 4d. on barley. A man farming 200 acres, bringing him in £225 a year gross, would have, it was reckoned, to pay out of this £20 for tithe, as well as £60 for rent and perhaps £80 for wages. Agricultural wages in most parts averaged rather over 1s. a day, supplemented by occasional emoluments in the way of food and drink and by boon-money in times of harvest. An unmarried labourer living with his employer's family received about £3 a year. In some parts of the country, as also at special seasons, agricultural labour was hired at piece-rates, many of the smaller proprietors adding to their income by occasional work for their richer neighbours. In Lancashire in 1664 ploughing was being paid for at 2s. 6d. a day, reaping at 1s. and haymaking at 6d. In many places labourers were still hired at Mop or Statute Fairs, where they stood in the market-places holding the implements of their craft—a carter his whip, a woodman his bill and a labourer his shovel. It was in such a manner that Gabriel Oak took service two centuries later.[4]

Though the state of the roads in winter limited the

* See a most interesting letter on this subject in the *Verney Memoirs*, ii (1925 ed.), 195-6.

size of every market and greatly enhanced the price of commodities in London, it was easy for a farmer to sell locally. Save for spices and a few luxuries foreign food was unknown, and there was a constant market not only for English corn and cattle, but for fruit, fowls, butter and cheese, in every country town. Here in ordinary seasons oxen of average quality fetched up to £5 apiece, cows up to £3, and sheep up to 10s. A cart-horse commanded from £8 to £15. Wheat averaged rather under 50s. a quarter, barley around 20s. and oats around 15s. Wool sold for between 9d. and 1s. a pound. These prices were of course subject to wide variations dependent on season, crop and place of market. But though country gentry and farmers sometimes grumbled in an " if corn and cattle bore as good a price as vest and tunic, 'tis probable better times might appear " manner, there was not much amiss with farming in the England of Charles II.[5]

Perhaps the most remarkable thing about English agriculture was its diversity. The great corn-lands were mostly in the east—in Cambridgeshire with its hedged fields and rows of willows, in Norfolk where the gentry exported their surplus wheat to Holland, and in Bedford and Huntingdonshire where every village was under the plough to feed the corn-markets of Bedford, St. Neots and Royston. The wheat of the south was sold at Farnham, whence it was borne on vast wagons carrying 40 bushel apiece to the mills on the Wey, and thence by barge to London; while that of Oxfordshire and Bucks passed through Aylesbury to be ground on the hill streams between Wycombe and Thames. There was good wheat too in the west, notably in Hertfordshire and Monmouth. The north grew no wheat or rye, but barley, peas, oats, beans and lentils. [6]

The finest grazing lands in England were Leicestershire, Lincolnshire and the Vale of Aylesbury. Norfolk too was famous for the black cattle that browsed in the meadows by Yare and Waveney, while its eastern marshes fattened the runts of the north which were driven there each year on their long trek to the London markets. The dairy-lands were Cheshire—the vale royal of England; High Suffolk, which sent its best butter to the capital in small firkins; North Wilts; and South Gloucestershire, famous for its soft, rich green cheese. The valleys of Severn and Wye, where fruit was so plentiful that any passer-by could pick it unhindered, were given over to hops and cider-apples, and those of northern Kent to hops and cherries. Sussex and Hampshire were rich in timber, drawn thence by oxen or floated down the southern rivers to the sea. [7]

The richest of England's agricultural products was her sheep. Though Leicestershire bred the largest for mutton, Cotswold, Wiltshire and Dorset upland, with their sweet and aromatic plants, raised the flocks whose wool fed the fine cloth trade of the south-west. In 1669 it was reckoned that 40,000 sheep grazed within three miles of Dorchester alone, while once a year graziers travelled from every part of the country to the great sheep-fair on lonely Weyhill above Andover town. And beside every road that crossed the chalk downlands of southern England were shepherds tending their flocks. [8]

These were the high-lights, but the glow from English farming was steadily diffused over the whole land. Black dray- and coach-horses from Leicestershire, turkeys and geese from Essex and Suffolk that marched each autumn Londonwards in armies along the eastern highways, poultry from sandy Surrey commons, and hogs fattened for bacon on the surplus whey and skimmed milk of Hampshire, helped to make little England as prosperous as she was beautiful. All over the world she was famed for her good fare: Besseleigh turnip and Derby ale, Hampshire honey, Tewkesbury mustard and Warwickshire ram! It is the glorious variety of it all that makes the old English husbandry so pleasant to contemplate. [9]

Yet seventeenth-century England was no longer a purely agricultural country. Trade, fostered by Puritan virtues, was all the time growing. The poverty that followed in the train of the Civil Wars stimulated this expansion, for it drove many Englishmen, whose early upbringing had accustomed them to a good standard of living, to seek a return on their reduced capital that only enterprise could give. The costly tastes which the restored Court imported from France aided the process. " Venturing " was in the very air.

When young Dudley North made his first voyage to the Levant as a Turkey apprentice, his lawyer brother invested the whole of his slender savings with him, while his father gave him a hundred pounds and bade him live on it and make his fortune. He did so, peer's younger son as he was; a life of wretched poverty would have been the only alternative. So also William Blundell of Crosby, struggling to keep his estates together under the pressure of fines and decimation, scraped together £40 and risked it in a small share of "an adventure to the Barbados in the good ship *Antelope* of Liverpool," to receive a year later a 100 per cent return on his investment. "Keep your shop and your shop will keep you," was the prudent motto of the London trader; but this steady integrity was given the fire of genius by a splendid capacity for taking risks. A city merchant told Pepys how by doing so he had had credit for £100,000 at a time when his total wealth in hand was not more than £1,000.[10]

Such were the beginnings of a new world capitalism which the English, above all other races, were to exploit, though they were as yet outdistanced in it by their rivals, the Dutch. The growth of luxurious tastes, with the consequent demand for products which could only be obtained at great cost, offered a premium to the trader who had the capital or credit to lay out on remote returns. But the process was in its infancy, and there was still scope for the small man with pluck and initiative. A universal spirit of enterprise prevailed, everyone being ready to supplement his earnings by setting up in some sort of trade. A foreign visitor in 1669 reported that there was not a rustic's cottage in Devon or Somerset that did not manufacture white lace; in Suffolk every housewife at open cottage door plied her rock and distaff, and in Gloucestershire the old women knitted stockings while they smoked their pipes or carried their puddings to the bakehouse.

With this industry went integrity of workmanship. Throughout the world the English were building up a reputation for quality of product.* It was symptomatic of their genius that they excelled in the making of instruments of precision. All this was founded on that homely and solid craftsmanship which had arisen in England out of the needs of the village. Every parish had its subsidiary population of masons, carpenters, smiths, wheelwrights, who made its houses and furniture, supplied its agricultural implements, shoed its horses and did its repairs. This rustic proximity of client to craftsman set a premium on thorough workmanship, which, handed down from father to son, survived in newer crafts where the local check was wanting. The typical English craftsman of the seven-

* "The English . . . through all the world are counted the most ingenious in all manner of manufactures as cloth, serge, woollen stockings, silk stockings, both woven and knitted, which I have seen transported to Naples, Messina, Palermo, all places whence silk is transplanted into England, all sorts of leather, scarlet cloth, gloves, watches, knives, etc."— Denis du Repos to Sir Edward Harley, 13 Sept., 1662, *H.M.C. Portland,* III, 328.

teenth century was such a man as old Jonas Shish, that plain, honest ship's carpenter, whom Evelyn knew, and who, though he could hardly read and never could explain his trade to another, built many a fine ship, as his forebears had done for generations before him.[11]

English mercantile enterprise was backed by the natural equipment of the country. With plenty of coal, iron, lead, lime and timber, and an easily accessible littoral, rich in harbours, she was ideally situated for world trade. Her chief commodity was her woollen manufactures, but she exported as well tin, pewter, brass, horn, leather, glass and earthenware. In return her merchants brought home tobacco from the plantations of the New World, wine from France, Spain and Portugal, sugar and rum from Barbados and Jamaica, spices and silks from the Levant, timber and tar from the Baltic, and cotton goods from India.

The Navigation Acts gave the carriage of most of these commodities to English shipowners, whose trade was passing more and more from the coastwise routes to those of the seven seas. Those who manned their vessels served a rough and varied apprenticeship, often beginning their sea-life in the fishing trade before they took service in the merchantmen, or more occasionally in the King's ships of war. All round the English coasts the shipbuilders were busy—at Newcastle, Sunderland, Hull, Yarmouth, Aldeburgh, Harwich, Shoreham, Portsmouth and Bristol—while the whole of the

Thames from London Bridge to Blackwall was a vast shipbuilding yard. And to feed the yards her rivers were filled with timber floating seawards from the more accessible woods.[12]

This sea-borne trade was paid for by a heavy price in human suffering. The merchant captains and seamen who trafficked with the Mediterranean ports took their lives in their hands, and suffered more perils than those of the Atlantic waves. From Sallee, Algiers and Tripoli issued the Moorish corsairs, with whose governments the English Crown lived at best in a state of precarious peace, and whose swift vessels were a match for all but the strongest of merchantmen. Many English seamen captured by them passed the remainder of their lives in loathsome captivity. Others after years were ransomed by the funds raised by the charitable in England for the redemption of slaves. So a tender-hearted gentleman wrote to the Secretary of the Admiralty to tell him how Captain Spurrill, who had endured nine years' cruel usage at Tangier, had been redeemed by his efforts. " And now this poor suffering man is free," he added, " if you will thrust him into his majesty's service that he may know how to live, I will publish your generosity to everybody."

Of the freights that English ships bore outwards, cloth was king. The three great districts of its manufacture were East Anglia, the south-west, and Yorkshire. From the former came the baizes and serges of Colchester and Sudbury, all the villages round which span wool for Portugal and Italy. Colchester in 1662 boasted eight fine churches and employed 10,000 workers. As one travelled from Suffolk to Norfolk the signs of industry and prosperity became still more marked, a face of diligence being spread over the whole country, till the spires of Norwich rose before one, the greatest town in England for the making of stuffs and worsted stockings.

In the south-west was the quality trade. This was the broadcloth manufacture, which clothed the fine gentlemen and rich merchants of half Europe. Fed by the wool of Salisbury Plain and the Cotswolds, almost every parish in the land between upper Thames and Exe was learning to make fine cloth. From the towns of four counties—Somerset, Wiltshire, Dorset and Gloucestershire—the master-clothiers sent out wool to the villages, where women and children span the yarn which later their packmen collected for their looms. Here the union, so strange to modern minds, of capitalism and cottage industry, was enriching a whole community. In the pleasant valleys of the Stroud and Wiltshire Avon the sides of the hills were covered with the paddocks of rich clothiers, each man in his fair stone house and spending his £500 a year. Bristol for drugget and cantaloon, Taunton for serges, Wells for fine Spanish stockings, Frome for medley cloth, and Bradford-on-Avon and Stroud for dyes, were the household names of the west-country trade that Bristol, Barnstaple and Blackwell Hall exported to all the world.

THE MEANS OF LIFE

And farther west was Exeter of the serges, where thousands of artisans and all the country-folk for twenty miles round were continuously employed in making baizes and light cloths for Spain, France, Italy and the Levant.

The cloth trade of the West Riding, which in the next century was to swallow up both her rivals, was as yet only concerned with the coarser manufactures. The narrow cloths or Yorkshire kerseys of Leeds, Halifax, Huddersfield, Bradford and Wakefield supplied the needs of common folk who could not afford the fine medley and broadcloth of the west. As population flowed from village to town, and the smaller parishes ceased to be self-supporting, this trade advanced with great strides; for the present it was still subsidiary to its rivals of the south. Yet the great wool market at Leeds that appeared miraculously twice a week down the broad main street of the town, was already resorted to by factors with letters from customers in places as distant as Russia and North America. It was fed by the hardy industry of the Yorkshire clothiers, whose houses and stony enclosures lined the slopes of the West Riding valleys, so that as one gazed down them the eye was caught by the pale gleam of innumerable pieces of white cloth stretched upon the tenters. With coal and running water at their doors, they were able to complete in their own houses almost all the processes required for their trade.

Besides the three cloth provinces other districts were

in part maintained by the clothing manufacture. Shrewsbury made white broadcloth and flannel, Kendal linsey-woolseys and cotton stuff for blankets, and Newbury shalloons for lining clothes. Stockings were woven throughout the eastern midlands, especially at Nottingham, Doncaster and Leicester. And the universal fashion of wearing lace kept many a Buckinghamshire housewife busy and well-to-do.[13]

All this manufacturing was rural in its setting, while most of those who practised it were engaged also in agriculture. The merchants and shopkeepers of the provincial towns kept farm and orchard in the adjacent meads. Only giant London, and to a lesser degree Bristol, were urban entities. The latter, with its crowded Tolsey, its tall bridge across the Avon lined like London's with continuous houses, and its cobbled stones worn smooth by sledges, was the only place in England beside the capital which could market unaided the goods which its merchants brought home. Its carriers supplied all South Wales, the south-west, and the western midlands with sugar, wine, oil and tobacco. Liverpool, which with the growth of the industrial north was to outdistance Bristol in the next century, was still only in process of transition from a ragged fishing-village to a brick town, while Southampton was dying of old age and the London competition.

Straw hats from Dunstable, saddles from Burford, buttons and thread from Maidstone, salt from Worcester, Chester and Newcastle, were some of the lesser manufactures which rustic England produced in the last age before the Industrial Revolution. The geographical distribution of industry is best indicated by the annual excise returns; that for 1665 shows that while London, Middlesex and Surrey were together farmed for £140,000, the yield for Yorkshire, Kent, Norfolk and Devon was £16,000, £15,000, £13,800, and £9,500 respectively, and for Essex, Gloucester, Suffolk and Lincolnshire from £8,600 to £7,200. None of the other counties was farmed for more than £4,600, with little Huntingdonshire, which was almost entirely rural, bringing up the rear with an excise rental of only £1,400.[14]

Coal, iron and steel, the industrial sinews of a later England, were still produced for domestic purposes only, though the Government occasionally offered subsidies for the export of coal. The old homes of the iron industry were Sussex and southern Surrey, where forests fed the charcoal furnaces. But with a growing shortage of timber in the more accessible forests the trade was beginning to move to the north. In Shropshire and Sherwood Forest water-power was already used to drive the forges, where with weighty hammers, bigger than any southern smith could handle, long bars of iron were beaten out. Yet it was symptomatic of that England that in the pools beside the forges there was store of good trout. Farther north the prosperous steel-masters of Sheffield covered all Hallamshire with the smoke of their old forges; their edged tools were known by their quality from the Volga to the Caribbean Sea.

Coal had long been mined in most of those districts where it is found to-day, but only near the sea, or where there was easy river transport, was anything but a local market available. Elsewhere the price was prohibitive. In time of war, when the great fleets of colliers from the Tyne were intercepted or blockaded, the price of coal in the capital would rise from around twenty shillings to four pounds or more a chaldron. In most parts of the country the people relied on other fuel than coal—on wood, with which the land still abounded, though it was felled so extravagantly that the far-sighted already prophesied a fuel famine; on turf from the moors, and mosses; and, in some districts where plantations were scarce, on cow-dung, which the country-people dried in summer and stacked in cakes against their walls against the winter. "It's a very offensive fuel," wrote a lady traveller.[15]

The lack of adequate roads, which kept English coal below ground, acted as a constant brake on commercial expansion. The highways were still as they had been in the Middle Ages, broad and ill-defined tracks winding across open country. The wheeled traffic, which the English in their passion for fast travelling now imposed on them, made their surfaces worse than ever. In winter the main roads became impassable seas of mud, so that travellers were forced to abandon them and invade the neighbouring fields.

Their measure is best taken by the fact that it was the usual practice of the parish authorities to plough the ruts up each spring with the road-plough that lived under the church porch.

In some parts of the country, notably in the heavy midlands and the deep clays of Sussex, teams of oxen were sometimes used to draw carts and coaches, and in the west the hills were so full of rolling stones and the lanes so narrow that corn was carried not in carts but on the backs of horses, corded on wooden frames. As the seventeenth century drew to a close the hungry demands of the metropolis turned every highway near it into a quagmire, sodden with the ordure of a never-ceasing procession of beasts—cattle, sheep, turkeys, geese—marching to the London slaughter-houses. And there were other terrors, begotten of human needs, for on every heath and moor suspicious-looking men, muffled up in great-coats and with pistols at their sides, might be observed as though speculating on the possible strength of passing travellers. Those who seemed to have small capacity for resistance they would approach and travel beside for a while, until opportunity offered for even closer acquaintance.

On such roads it was easy for travellers to lose their way. Signposts were almost unknown,* and it was a frequently observed phenomenon that the farther one

* That experienced traveller, Celia Fiennes, writing in the reign of William III, noted with astonishment a Lancashire experiment—"that at all crossways there are posts with hands pointing to each road with the names of the great town or market town that it leads to."—*Fiennes*, 157.

journeyed from London the longer and more irregular became the intervals between the milestones. On the lonelier stretches travellers hired guides; Pepys, riding from Huntingdon to Biggleswade, was forced to employ the services of two countrymen to lead him through the waters that enflanked and invaded the road. At every few miles travellers were forced to ford a stream, and at every few hundred yards to circumvent a watercourse. Bridges were few, and many of the broader rivers could only be crossed by ferry,* an unpleasant proceeding which necessitated maddening delay, and often, in winter, a severe cold.[16]

But the inns on the main highways were excellent and travellers could usually look for blazing fires and plenty of warm food and drink. From famous houses like " The Bull " at St. Albans to village inns like that thrice-blessed one at Withington in the Cotswolds, where Thomas Baskerville found " excellent ale, a conscionable landlord " and a night's fare and lodging for seven persons, all for seventeen shillings, the standard was the highest in Europe. Innkeeping in England was regarded as a respectable, and even honourable profession; at the " Crown," Mansfield, the landlord and his wife were gentlefolk. More often the former was " an honest ingenious man " of the middle rank, who distilled incomparable strong waters and kept good wine, a bowling-green and perhaps a cockpit for

* That over the Mersey, which carried a hundred people and horses at a time, took an hour and a half in the passage.—*M. Blundell,* Cavalier.

his neighbours. In many places after the Restoration he was an old merry soldier, who had fought for King Charles and loved to regale travellers with tales of Prince Rupert and Marston Moor. And since horses and inns went together, he was generally something of a jockey, and, like good Mr. Hunt of the " Three Cranes," Doncaster, was fond of riding and talking of horses. And with such comfort for mind and body, it mattered little if an odd frog or two croaked in one's chamber, or if mine host, anxious not to foul more sheets than necessary, was over-apt to assume that his guests were ready to share a bed.[17]

But if there were compensations on the roads for travellers, there were few for trade. A single man by riding post might cover the distance from Huntingdon to London in the inside of a day, or from Chester to London in two, but anything heavier was doomed to ceaseless delay. Even the much-advertised " flying coaches," which, first appearing in this reign, accomplished the journey from Oxford to the " Greyhound " in Holborn in a single day, never failed to conclude their printed bills with the cautious proviso, " If God permit." And, miraculous as their speed appeared to contemporaries, they were still slow enough: four days in summer and six in winter were allowed for the " flying coaches " from the capital to York. Heavy goods, if they journeyed by land, did so without reference to time, and if they were perishable journeyed not at all. Hence it was that mackerel could be bought at a penny a hundred on the beach at Bridport, and yet fetch twice as many shillings in the London market. Long strings of pack-horses, travelling in file with a bell tinkling from the leading horse, were the goods trains of that age; coal, iron, wool and crates of clay for the potteries all travelled in this way. In many parts of the country narrow stone causeways, raised above the morass of the surrounding highway, were being built to accommodate such traffic.[18]

One commodity in England travelled quickly—His Majesty's mails. Ever since the Crown had taken over the responsibility for a postal service at the beginning of the century the speed at which letters moved had been increasing. Each of the main roads radiating from London had its regular service, with post-houses at all the principal towns. Here letters were distributed to the local carriers or fetched by the messengers of the country gentry; it was important in addressing to put the right superscription. "Pray," wrote a Lancashire squire to a London correspondent, "forget not Liverpool, for your last two letters being directed to Preston (20 miles off north of the road) came late to my hand."

Letters were charged on delivery, and by the sheet and distance: a single sheet travelled from London for twopence for the first eighty miles, and a double sheet for twice as much; those who were extravagant in their use of paper were apt to be unpopular with their correspondents. Envelopes being unknown, letters were elaborately folded, sealed and addressed on the outside, as

> " To my honourable Friend
> Sir Jeffrey Shakerley
> at his house Hulme
> Stone bag."

Sometimes, especially in the case of Government dispatches, they were further superscribed with directions to local postmasters and postboys, "Haste, haste, haste," there was scrawled across one letter which aroused much excitement as it travelled down the Great North Road, "for his Majesty's most important service. Ride for your life."

The chief drawback of the postal service was its cost. An unsuccessful scheme of 1659, and a successful one of 1680, attempted to overcome this by the establishment of a penny post in the capital. That of 1680, which gave immortality to a not too reputable speculator named Dockwra, first introduced the principle of dated postmarks, which are to be found on London letters after that year. As, however, it infringed the Government's monopoly, the scheme was taken over by the State, which incorporated most of its other features but characteristically doubled the cost. But the high cost of postage was in part overcome by the privilege of franking, allowed to members of both Houses of Parliament. As legislators were exceedingly generous in providing their friends and constituents with signatures,* few merchants of importance had any difficulty in getting their letters franked.[19]

Since the roads were so bad, much of the heavier merchandise travelled by river. Thus the wharves of Reading, Maidenhead and Henley shipped Berkshire and Oxfordshire malt and meal on to the barges which fed London, taking in return oils, groceries, salt and tobacco for the neighbouring countryside. Every sizable river bore its share of freightage, and as the century drew to a close scheme after scheme came before Parliament for making navigable some provincial river and opening up new trade.[20]

The quiet years of Charles II's reign, between the Civil Wars that had passed and the great wars with France to come, were marked by steady mercantile and colonial expansion. Men were laying up for themselves and their children treasure for the future. On every sea the adventurous ships of England sailed, returning with riches in their holds to enhance the wealth of a little island of squires, yeomen and homely merchants, and bringing silks and scents and delicate cloths for their ladies. In a quarter of a century Evelyn's £250 invested in the stock of the East India Company multiplied itself threefold. Pennsylvania, whither Charles had dispatched the Quaker Penn in 1682; the Carolinas, New York and the shores of the Hudson;

---

* Among the Shakerley correspondence is a pained letter from a postal official to a Member of Parliament complaining of the excessive number of letters that travelled free in his name, and asking sadly how he contrived to write from so many places at the same time.

treaties with the Turks and the Moors to make Englishmen free of the Mediterranean; trading settlements at
Bombay and Fort William, and dusky ambassadors
bringing gifts from the great Mogul; companies to
trade with Africa, Guinea and the coasts of Barbary;
expeditions to find a new road to the golden East
through the Arctic ice or discover the wonders of the
South Seas: all these were milestones in England's
commercial and imperial expansion, and all, in their
greater or lesser degree, bore the impress of a king who
once told his sister: " The thing which is nearest the
heart of this nation is trade and all that belongs to it."

This is no place to speak of the work of the English
colonial pioneers of the latter seventeenth century, yet
the spirit of them is the essence of that England. There
was romance in it, and there was courage: romance,
for those who sailed to the plantations entered a
world of enchantment where anything might happen
—death in a raging fever, or the miracle that attends
the youngest and disinherited sons of kings in fairy
stories.* There was confidence too—supreme and
immeasurable—in what a little nation of 5,000,000
could achieve. " This part of Africa is very fertile,"
wrote an English pioneer with all Nubia lying before

* In 1670 there appeared in the city of London a rich East Indian merchant
of some twenty-seven years of age. Visiting the sights of the town, he
chanced on Bedlam, and there, opening one of the hutches to view a
lunatic, was hailed by the distracted woman within as her long-lost bastard
son, " By the same token," she said, " that he had a spot on his shoulder
and left buttock." Examination proved the truth of her story, the young
man having been kidnapped for the plantations in infancy, leaving her
bereft of her senses.

him, "and wants nothing but English industry to improve it." Trade followed romance. [21]

The atmosphere of adventure and intellectual curiosity was favourable to scientific discovery. During the Interregnum a little group of men, sickened by fanatic extravagances, had begun to meet in Wadham College to discover something of the world they lived in. They were the nucleus of the Royal Society, which was founded in Christopher Wren's room in Gresham College shortly after the Restoration. At their weekly meetings the conversation was philosophical and cheerful, and the experiments ranged all nature. They employed an itinerant, who each year made a report of his discoveries in England, bringing back not tales of new Messiahs or godly judgments on the wicked, but dried fowls and fish, plants and minerals. When 'rince Rupert was about to lead a fleet against the Dutch on the Guinea coast the virtuosos requested him to employ his leisure in sounding the depths without a line and fetching up water from the bottom of the sea. In their boundless curiosity they were laying the foundations of the modern world. Even in death's dark vale, when the Plague was at its height, Evelyn, calling at Durdans, discovered Dr. Wilkins, Sir William Petty and Mr. Hooke contriving chariots, new rigging for ships, a wheel to run races in, and other mechanical inventions. [22]

Pneumatic engines, aeolipiles for weighing air, calculating machines, quench-fires, even a "new

fashion gun to shoot off often, one after another,
without trouble or danger, very pretty," all came alike
to this remarkable generation. In our own age of
marvels, but dimly understood, we are standing, as
Newton said of himself, on the shoulders of giants.
And with all this achievement these men were not
specialists, but versatile beyond our imagination.
Wren, at twenty-four, was a Professor of Astronomy
and the wonder of Europe for mechanical invention,
and was over thirty before he ever thought of archi-
tecture. The learned Lord Keeper Guilford, beside
attaining to an exquisite skill in music, devoted much
time to the Torricellian experiments; his youngest
brother, Roger North, barrister, musician, author and
architect, mastered the theory of light. "The very
remembrance of these things," he wrote in after years,
"is delight, and while I write methinks I play. All
other employments that filled my time go on account
of work and business: these were all pleasure."[23]

All this travels a long way from the sober paths of
national livelihood, yet the two were closely allied. To
scoffers it may have seemed that the virtuosos, seated
civilly on the rising benches that faced the famous green
cloth table in Gresham College, were occupied solely
with such concerns as collecting the eyes of oysters and
the galls of doves, and generally of "finding the north-
west passage into the land of philosophy." More
observant people saw the practical nature of their
researches; the Frenchman Sorbière reported how

their members " built laboratories, made machines, opened mines, and made use of an hundred sorts of artists to find out some new invention or other." It was this, the shrewd Gaul foresaw, that in a future age was to give England the commercial leadership of the world.[24]

In all this activity of the English breadwinner there was little hindrance from the State. The old restraints of the medieval corporate State survived in theory rather than in practice, and were everywhere falling into disuse. Taxes, after the crushing exactions of the Interregnum, were low, and direct taxation, save in time of war, almost negligible. Most of the royal revenue was raised by the indirect impositions of Customs and Excise, and the former protected English industry quite as much as the latter penalised it. And wherever Customs duties proved excessive they were mitigated by the wholesale smuggling that immediately sprang up, for in those policeless days the laws of supply and demand easily overrode the paternal intentions of governments. On Romney Marsh the illicit export of wool (which was called " owling ") and the import of brandy, wine and tobacco proved so profitable that it maintained a whole population of armed smugglers, fully capable of intimidating the occasional soldiers sent to suppress them.[25]

For the rest, wages and prices were reasonably well proportioned to the earnings and needs of the nation. An artisan could earn from 10s. to 20s. a week. A pound of the best beef, mutton or veal could be bought in town for 3d., of sweet new butter for 6d. and of good cheese for 2d. A fat pig cost around 30 shillings and flitch bacon 4d. a pound. To wash such fare down a flagon of strong draught ale was to be had for 2d. in good times and 3d. in bad, and beer in the bottle for 6d. a dozen; in the cider counties prime red streak sold for 6d. a quart. For grander folk sack and claret were obtainable in ordinary times at 4s. a gallon, though war or embargo might treble the price in a week. With this must be remembered the difficulty of obtaining commodities out of season and in a bad year. [26]

The etceteras of life were more expensive. A pound of single rush candles cost 5d., a great deal of money for such a little illumination—a fact which explains the universal habit of the poor of rising at dawn and going to bed at sundown. And luxuries were still dearer: silver was around 6s. an ounce, while a small tapestry tablecloth cost 15s. or 16s. A lady furnishing a country house had to pay over £1. 16s. a yard for blue damask, while the gilded fringes demanded by fashion were even more expensive. And the kind of books an educated man would read were utterly beyond the reach of the poor; Dugdale's *St. Paul's*, a small folio, unbound and in sheets, cost 14s. 6d., a sum equivalent to at least £6 in present-day money. [27]

It is instructive to compare the payment of highly skilled artificers and professional men with these prices.

A barber, who was still somewhat of an occasional luxury, charged from 6d. for a hair-cut, 1s. for bleeding, and for regular shaving operations (usually once a week) around 3s. a quarter; a silversmith for cutting a coat of arms on a tankard 3s., and a music master for teaching two little girls the harpsichord £1 a month. A country artist would paint a portrait for £5 (the fashionable London article was of course far more expensive). The salaries of the professors at Oxford and Cambridge ranged with one or two exceptions from £100 to £200 a year, that of the Clerk of the Acts of the Navy was £400, of the chaplain and physician of the Tangier garrison £182 10s. and £273 15s. respectively. To these latter were added, it should be remembered, perquisites—for those in the swim as good a method of getting rich quickly in that day as inspired speculation in stocks and shares in our own.[28]

Judged by modern standards, the cost of clothes was the heaviest item in the budget of a seventeenth-century English man or woman. There were two reasons for this. Light, washable fabrics were little used; clothes were meant to endure and were made of material correspondingly expensive. Even when their day was over, the stuff of which they were made was turned to other purposes; many a great lady cut up her own and her husband's fine clothes to make the covers which still adorn their descendants' chairs and stools, while Mr. Pepys went abroad in a faced white

coat made of his wife's petticoat. And clothes in that
age notified status: a fine embroidered coat marked
the gentleman, fustian the yeoman, and so on. Men
and women were therefore prepared to pay heavy
prices for the popular respect their garments earned;
gold and silver lace were universal passports. Nor,
since the means of safe investment were still very
limited, did men mind sinking large sums of capital in
their wardrobes: £100 on one's back was at least as
safe as a £100 on loan to the Exchequer. In the highest
circles of the Court small fortunes were sunk in this
way; at the coronation of Charles II the Duke of
Buckingham spent £30,000.

Even for ordinary occasions of fashion the expendi-
ture on clothes was high. To put himself in a " handsome posture " a gentleman would have to pay for
coat, breeches and doublet not less than £7 or £8—
at least £100 in the language of 1960—and another £3
for lace cravat and ruffles. Then there was the sword—
de rigueur for anyone who wanted to be smart—which,
suitably gilded, would run the bill up by a further £2,
with a hat at £1 and a silver hat-band at another 15s.
Such minor items as shoes cost around 4s. a pair, silk
stockings 11s., and fine fringed gloves 15s. Fine
ladies were still more expensive to dress. A modish
grey night-gown alone could cost £5 5s. But the
show they and their male company must have made
must have been worth it. Flowered satin dress, and
yellow petticoat, or ribboned gown of black gimp lace,

was matched by fine doublet cloak and waistcoat, with buttons and trimmings of silver and gold, all in the brilliant colours of the rich deep dyes for which England was famous. Those who to-day have held their breath at the beauty of half a dozen scarlet coats against the russet background of an English park can form some slight impression of the coloured kaleidoscope of seventeenth-century life.

Descriptions of dress are generally tedious and are best made brief. A gentleman of Charles II's day wore a loose hanging surcoat decorated but unfastened by gold buttons, a waistcoat tied to his body by a sash and a band or cravat of lace. Beneath were broad beribboned breeches, silk stockings of the same colour, and low shoes with high heels and buckles, over which were drawn, when he donned his cloak and called for his horse, top-boots and woollen or leather riding-stockings. The head was crowned by a vast, dark, curling periwig, on which when out of doors there sailed, as on a heraldic sea, a low hat with a broad brim and a bow on one side. A good periwig cost about £2, and one of the shorter wigs for riding or undress less; there was a great demand for the fashionable texture and colour, and country girls with hair of the right colour could earn good money by selling their superfluous locks. Ladies also affected perukes of fair hair (Pepys was mad when his wife donned one), with enticing fringes and curls called " puffs," gloves perfumed with jasmine or rosecake, and a great deal of lace—laced gowns, whisks, aprons, petticoats and even shoes.

In the country both sexes went abroad in rougher and cheaper wear; a decent shag coat could be had for 25s. and a black shalloon suit for under £3. The plain gentry of the shires mostly ordered their own cloth and then paid a local tailor to make it up. Sir Geoffrey Shakerley bought three yards of broadcloth for a suit and coat for £1 14s. The Rev. Giles Moore of Horstead Keynes in Sussex tells us how he disposed of three and three-quarter yards of scarlet serge purchased for 15s., " of which I made the library carpet besides my waistcoat." Humbler folk in the villages span flax and wool at home to make their own clothes: a Lancashire farmer's breeches were made of two calves' skins for half a crown. But even among the poorest there was plenty of colour: the country-women in the eastern counties wore red petticoats and waistcoats, crowned with straw hats. In the towns the populace was largely clad in the colours and clothes of their different callings: thus parsons wore black and butchers and tallow chandlers blue.

For the poor the outer garments alone sufficed. Beneath them and in their beds they wore nothing. But the rich were not without underlinen. Sir Robert Harley, in his inventory of fine holland shirts, woollen stockings and fustian waistcoats, mentions the possession of two pairs of drawers, and Mrs. Pepys, as her husband's jealous record tells, occasionally wore the same. The learned Anthony Wood paid 2s. for " a pair of woollen loinings," and Randle Neild lost a bellyband valued at 6d. And ladies then as now were most particular about their shifts and petticoats; those of Nell Gwynne gave the utmost satisfaction to a French ambassador privileged to view them. " There is nothing," wrote the same nice observer, " neater than the feet and ankles of the English ladies in their well-fitting shoes and silk stockings. They wear their skirts short, and I often see legs so well turned that a sculptor would like to mould them. The garter, of which glimpses are often afforded, is below the knee, and in black velvet with diamond buckles. Those who have no silk stockings to wear show a white skin smooth as satin." [29]

CHAPTER VII

THE ENGLISH POLITY

THE government of this England rested on triple supports—Crown, Law and People. The Crown was the Executive and provided the element of decisive power which is needed from time to time in all government. But it was a carefully tempered power, and the unpopularity which generally attaches to Executive government was modified by the hallowed place which the Crown held in the English heart. The very pomp and colour which hedged it about helped to support it; its appeal was to the deepest emotions of the race.

The home of the Executive was the old Palace of Whitehall. For nearly half a mile it stretched beside the river, a warren of galleries, apartments and gardens, the home not only of the King but of the Ministers of State, servants high and low, courtiers, chaplains, ladies and all the gilded army which encompassed the English throne. One entered it either from the river or the lane—that " long dark dirty and very inconvenient passage "—which, spanned by two gateways, linked Charing Cross with Westminster. Its buildings were of all sizes and ages, from the classic Banqueting Hall to the little octagonal Cockpit.[1]

The centre of this courtly city was the long Stone Gallery, the very hub of the Stuart Government of Britain. On its walls hung the pictures which Charles I had collected and his enemies dispersed, and which his son had partly reassembled. Here they made a kind of National Picture Gallery, for the place was open to all comers. Yet few in the crowd that walked continuously up and down the Galleries came for the pictures; places, preferment, sightseeing—above all, news—were the ceaseless business of that place of rumours. " It runs through the Galleries," was the prefix which sped the national gossip.[2]

Well it might, for those who waited here saw the outward stir of all that was moving the wheels of State. The velvet curtains across the doors would part and the King himself pass through the crowd, followed by a group of ministers and suitors from Bedchamber or Council Room, still contending for that royal ear, whose retention was at once the hardest and most precious achievement of a careerist's life. Here in the Gallery, for a moment, opportunity flitted by.[3]

From the Stone Gallery guarded doors opened into the royal apartments. In the Robes and Council Chambers the great committees of State sat in debate, while in the Withdrawing-room the waiting gentlemen warmed their hands before the fire. Beyond was the holy of holies, the Bedchamber. In this great room, with its windows looking on to the tides and shipping of the river, the most secret affairs of State were transacted at all hours of the day " between the bed and the wall ".[4]

It was not here, or in his closet, that England saw its King, nor even in the Ante-room where the Foreign Ministers daily awaited his return from the park, but in perfumed Banqueting Hall and Chapel. He dined in state, a little after midday, before a background of tapestry, while the massed lords of the household served him on bended knee, and all England came and went in the galleries above to share the pageantry. For the palace against whose background the high mysteries of State were set was a public property in which all shared. One must picture the national Executive in a setting of crimson and gold, with the royal trumpeters and kettledrummers marching in scarlet cloaks with facings of silver lace, before tapestries and fringed hangings, glorious gilt mirrors and a world of gleaming fabric.[5]

A few hundred yards down the muddy lane called King Street and across the cobblestones of Palace Yard was the Parliament House. Here sat the watchdog set by the nation to prevent the royal Executive from overriding the law. At least that was how the great bulk of the nation saw it, for the theory of Parliamentary sovereignty, first put forward by the extremists of the iron time, had been abandoned at the Restoration as repugnant to the English Constitution and habit: the old view of England was that Parliaments met at Westminster, not to govern, but to prevent others from misgoverning. The age of Charles II was the last age in which this was so; after 1688, when the people's representatives became themselves the governors of the nation, the people lost the ancient buffer between themselves and the Executive.

Before the English Revolution the power of King and Parliament alike was subjected to the rule of established law. It was to this indefinable and largely unwritten body of legal sanctions—" the known law of the land "—that both parties appealed in the Civil War. When the soldiers and parliamentary extremists set up an entirely new form of government that took no account of customary law the national conscience was outraged. The Restoration was brought about by the almost universal desire of the people to recover the ancient laws—the inherited safeguard of their lives and property—which alone they felt could protect them from the tyranny alike of profiteers and of irresponsible theorists. In one sense King and Parliament were nothing more to the people than the machinery for the proper working of the rule of law.

Parliament was not democratic. It represented not the masses but the privileged estates of the realm—those, in fact, who were best able to safeguard ancient legal rights against an encroaching Executive. The House of Commons was composed mainly of country magnates, with a sprinkling of merchants, officials and courtiers. They were chosen by a curious blend of nomination and limited election which varied from locality to locality; it was never very easy to say who had the right to vote and who had not. Their sittings were still spasmodic; twice in Charles II's reign long periods passed without any assembly at Westminster at all, and, for all the palaver made by a few ambitious politicians* at the time and by constitutional theorists since, there is little evidence that the country as a whole much resented the omission. It was only when the nation was in trouble that Parliament was ardently desired. Its chief power lay in its right to withhold those additional aids to the customary income of the Crown without which the Executive could scarcely afford to embark on any new policy. Throughout the seventeenth century, owing to the decline in the value of money, the Crown was persistently in need of such additional aid, and to this factor, more perhaps than to any other, must be set the destruction of the ancient balance between the Estates of the Realm on which the old polity of England was based.[6]

Though King, noble and landed magnate in Parliament alike ruled by hereditary right, England herself was democratic. For the unit of government was not Whitehall or Westminster, but the village. And here the feudal principle still obtained. The basis of

---

* "They like a flood break down all," was the comment of a quiet Englishman of the day on these talkative gentlemen.—*Verney Memoirs*, II, 374.

feudalism was that the tenure of property gave rise to inescapable civic obligations. The chief of these was the duty of taking an active part in the business of government. In the towns and among the nobility and gentry the feudal system was already dead or dying, and the rule of Cash and Credit had risen in its place. But in the villages, still virtually isolated in the long winter months, the feudal principle provided the administrative machinery of government.

The great county officials—the Sheriff and the Constables of the Hundreds, the Lord Lieutenant and his Deputies, the Justices sitting on their Bench of Quarter Sessions—provided the link between the distant Executive at Whitehall and the villages where the majority of English people lived. But the dog's work of government was carried out in the villages themselves. Those who did that work were drawn from the general body of the people. Every householder, who was not a member of one of the small classes specially exempted by Parliament from such service, was compelled to serve his turn in one of the parish offices or to provide an efficient substitute. And, since few could afford to pay for the latter, the average male citizen was more or less certain at least once in his life to hold executive office. Service was usually for a period of one year; it was unpaid and it was obligatory. Failure to perform its duties adequately was punishable at law by fine and imprisonment.

The principal parish officers were the Churchwardens, the Overseers of the Poor, the Overseers of the Highways, and the Petty Constables. The first, in addition to their modern duties of church maintenance, performed certain moral functions, such, for instance, as that of visiting the village ale-houses during the hour of divine service and driving malingerers to church. But in the seventeenth century the importance if not the dignity of the Churchwardens was already on the decline. The duties of the Overseers of the Poor were more onerous. Appointed by the Justices from a rota of householders, they were required to administer the Elizabethan Poor Law that made each parish responsible for the support of its own poor. It was their business to give weekly relief to the aged and impotent, to keep a stock of raw material on which to set the able-bodied unemployed to work, to build houses on the common land for the houseless, to educate poor children and bind them as apprentices, and to administer any lands or moneys left by the charitable for the poor of the parish. To provide for such services the Overseers were empowered to levy a Poor Rate under cover of the signature of the local Justices; for failure to perform them adequately they could be (and sometimes were) indicted at Quarter Sessions. It is just to add that our ancestors' attitude towards public assistance was little encumbered by sentiment: those in need of it were divided for administrative purposes into three classes—those who were seeking work, those who were unable to work, and those who could work but wouldn't: these last, the law enacted, were to be whipped as sturdy rogues and vagabonds, sent home to their own parishes and there set to work compulsorily. Yet neglect of a destitute person might bring the Overseers to the dock for manslaughter; while extravagance in the use of parish funds inevitably exposed them to the wrath of their neighbours. It was a salutary training in democracy, educating successive generations of the community in the business of administration.

Every parish was responsible for the upkeep of its own roads, and for providing an officer each year to see that the work was done. This functionary, called officially the Surveyor of the Highways, or more usually Boonmaster or Waywarden, had to carry out a task that called for much tact and could only too easily involve him in unpleasant relations with his neighbours. Appointed by the Court of Quarter Sessions from a list of agricultural holders submitted by the Vestry, it was his business during his year of office to see that all whose property adjoined the public highways kept clear their gutters and drains, trimmed their hedges and refrained from stacking their manure, timber or hay on the road. If they were refractory it was his duty to name them in the parish church after sermon, giving them thirty days' notice to make amends, after which he was entitled to do so himself at their expense. It was also his duty to waylay passing carts and wagons with more than the statutory number

166

of horses or wheels of less than the statutory width, and generally to enforce the transport enactments of Parliament and Privy Council. And three times a year he " viewed " every road, watercourse, pavement and bridge in the parish and reported their state to the Justices, subsequently, with the latters' authority, levying a highway rate to bear the cost of repairs. But his most arduous duty was the supervision of the statute labour which every householder either in person or by deputy was compelled by law to perform for six days in the year.

Such a power in the hands of a petty official as ill-educated as the average Surveyor might easily have been tyrannically used to gratify personal malice or pride in authority. It seldom was. For though the Surveyor was not subject to the surveillance of any popularly elected assembly, he had to bear a criticism far more formidable—that of his neighbours, among whom at the end of his year of office he had again to take his place. It was this which more than anything else prevented the existence of real despotism in that old England. Even the squire was, in a sense, subject to it. Justice of the Peace and lord of many acres though he might be, he was forced during many months of the year to seek his daily companionship among the humble folk who were his only accessible neighbours—the witnesses of all his actions and the lifelong judges of his conduct. Few men care to flout such opinion.

Apart from the small fry of parish officialdom—Clerk, Sexton, Beadle and Bellman—most of whom were paid, there was one other unpaid village officer, the greatest and oldest of all, the Constable. The Petty Constable was the policeman of the nation, and it was in keeping with the liberty-loving bent of the race that he was an amateur. He was appointed at the Court Leet and sworn by the Justices, and from the very first day of his office was made aware of the majesty of the law whose embodiment he had now for a season become.

> " You shall " (ran the oath given to the Constables of a northern shire) " exercise your office of Constable for the township of . . . and well and truly present all manner of bloodsheds, assaults, affrays and outcrys there done and committed against the King's Majesty's peace. All manner of writs, warrants and precepts to you lawfully directed you shall truly execute; the King's Majesty's peace in your own person you shall conserve and keep as much as in you lyeth. And in all other things that appertain to your office you shall well and truly behave yourself. So help you God and the content of this book."

At that majestic moment (it usually occurred on the rough paved floor of the local Courthouse) the mantle of many centuries of ordered peace fell on the shoulders of this humble man.

First and foremost, under the supervision of the Justices, it was the Constable's duty to preserve the King's peace. If any affray was made he was at once to proceed to the spot and, bearing his staff of Office, call upon the offenders to preserve that peace without which every man's hand was against every man's, and life, in the words of the seventeenth-century philosopher, " solitary, poor, nasty, brutish and short." It was a duty not unaccompanied by risk; " Christopher Stubbs of Wath," runs the record of a north-country Court, " presented at Richmond for making an assault and affray (on Christmas last in John Tanfield's house) on one John Stapleton and also for abusing James Harrison, Constable of Wath, reviling him and pulling away a great part of his beard, when commanding the said Christopher to keep the peace." In the pursuance of such a sacred duty the Constable could call on any citizen to assist, and it was an indictable offence to refuse to do so. For in the old England democracy was not a right but an obligation.

The Petty Constable's functions were so many that it must have been difficult for him during his year of office to earn his own livelihood. He was constantly dancing attendance on the Justices, before whom he had to bring malefactors for trial, being personally responsible for their safe keeping in the meantime: if there was no parish cage or lock-up, he had perforce to keep them in his own house. He had to execute the writs and warrants issued by the Justices, though an action lay against him at the suit of any injured person if in doing so he exceeded the law or trespassed on some private liberty—an inconvenience which none the less taught thousands of simple Englishmen who served their turn each year as parish constable the nature of English law. It must sometimes have been a relief to the Constable's feelings to execute the corporal punishments meted out by the Justices to erring citizens—to put a nagging woman in the ducking-stool, whip a sturdy rogue, or affix such a notice as Robert Storr and Christopher Smith, Constables of Bedale, were ordered to attach to the person of Margery Metcalf of Crackall: " I sit here in the Stocks for beating my own mother."

It was the Constable's duty, too, to supervise the statutes which an occasionally paternal Parliament passed against the rustic relaxations of cursing and swearing, tippling in ale-houses, profaning the Sabbath, and eavesdropping at neighbours' windows. In such matters custom and the remoteness of the central authority allowed him a wide discretion. Where a law or ordinance was likely to press too hardly, it was seldom enforced, a tacit understanding existing between Justice, Constable and citizen that in such a matter Crown and Parliament were better forgotten, at least in one parish, whatever might be the case elsewhere. This inefficiency, shocking as it must seem to modern minds, was compensated for by a salutory elasticity: hard and fast rules, with all their cold inhumanity, were everywhere eschewed: and the law, rough and cruel as it often was, was never far divorced from public opinion, on which it depended not for its making but for its enforcement. Neither Justice nor Constable was likely to enforce a law that outraged the good sense of the majority of his neighbours.

Most educative of all the parish Constable's tasks was his constant attendance at the County Courts and assemblies—at one time to present an offender at Petty Sessions, at another to wait on the Head Constable of the Hundred to present a return or pay in the parish taxes, while at every meeting of Quarter Sessions he had to journey to the shire town to answer an indictment brought against his village for failure of some statutory duty or listen to the charge of the magistrates. This brought at least one member of the village community each year into contact with a wider world, showed him how public business should be executed and taught him the practical difficulties of administration. It secured, what our vaunted system of democracy by numerical election too often fails to secure, a broad consent to the exactions of government from the plain citizen; for the latter felt that he himself shared in that government and knew its needs and difficulties. [7]

Such was the nursery of England's democracy. Her people were proud and independent, accustomed to manage their own affairs and resentful of interference. When a lord of the Court tried to keep the common folk of Windsor out of the Great Park they assembled in force, broke gates and pales and announced that the park was their own. Every fellow with a ragged cloth coat to his back felt that he had a part in the splendour and privilege of the great, and was ready to claim cousinhood with some titled magnate or ancient house; their honours, he felt, rested on his consent. Foreign visitors were always testifying to the rough strength of English democracy; the King, wrote Sorbière, had to be free and easy with the nobility, the officers of the Army with their soldiers, the landlords with their tenantry. There could be no government in the island on any other terms.

One sees the men of that age through the mists of time, upon which they cast gigantic and now perhaps unbelievable shadows—the hot-blooded gentry who fought in their cups, the country tenants twisting words in their manor courts to cheat their lords, the unpoliced Londoners who plundered the very sweetmeats from the feasts of the great. Proud and unbending, their natures were often tinged by melancholy and deep feeling that turned their pugnacity to strange enthusiasms and stranger oddities. "Everywhere in England," wrote a foreigner, " you will meet with gloomy and fanatical humours, presumption and extravagance of thought." Yet, there was something in them, he added, that was great and which they seemed to retain from the old Romans. It was from their freedom that they derived it. [8]

LIST OF ABBREVIATIONS USED

Bell, W. G. The Great *Fire* of London. 1920.

Blundell, M. Cavalier. 1933.

Bramston, Sir John. Autobiography of. 1845.

Brown, Thomas. The Works of. 3 vols. 1707–8.

Carte MSS. Carte MSS. in the Bodleian Library, Oxford.

Chamberlayne, Edward. Angliae Notitia. 1671 ed.

Cosmo, Grand Duke of Tuscany. Travels of. 1821.

C.S.P.D. Calandars of State Papers, Domestic Series (1660–81). 22 vols. 1860–1921.

Defoe, Daniel. Tour (ed. G. D. H. Cole. 2 vols. 1927).

Evelyn, John. Memoirs. 3 vols. 1906.

Fiennes, C. Through England on a Side Saddle in the Time of William and Mary. 1888.

Fleming. The Flemings in Oxford. (ed. J. R. Magrath). Vol. 1, 1903.

Forneron. Louise de Kéroualle.

Hatton Correspondence. Camden Society. 2 vols. 1878.

H.M.C. Reports of the Historical *MSS.* Commission.

Howell, J. Londinopolis. 1657.

Jusserand, J. J. A French Ambassador at the Court of Charles II. 1892.

King, Gregory. Natural and Political Observations upon the State and Condition of England. 1696.

North, Roger. The Lives of the Norths. 3 vols. 1890.

Pepys. Memoirs of Samuel (ed. H. B. Wheatley). 10 vols. 1893–9.

Ponsonby, Arthur. English Diaries. 1923.

Prideaux, Humphrey Letters of. (Camden Society.) 1875.

Rawlinson MSS. Rawlinson MSS. in Bodleian Library.

Reresby, Sir John. The Memoirs of (ed. Cartwright). 1875.

Rogers, J. E. Thorold. History of Agriculture and Prices in England. Vol. VI. 1887.

Rules of Civility, The. 1678.

Savile, Henry. Letters. (Camden Society.) 1857.

Shakerley MSS.

Sorbière, S. de. A Voyage to England. 1664.

Tanner, J. R. Further Correspondence of Samuel Pepys. 1929.

Teonge, Henry. The Diary of (ed. G. E. Manwaring). 1927.

Thurloe, John. A Collection of the State Papers of. 7 vols. 1742.

Traill, H. D. (ed.). Social England. Vol. IV. 1895.

Trotter, E. Trotter, *Seventeenth Century Life in the Country Parish.* 1919.

Verney Memoirs. 2 vols. 1925 ed.

Williamson, Sir Joseph. Letters addressed to. (Camden Society.) 2 vols. 1874.

Wood, Anthony. The Life and Times of. 5 vols. 1891.

Wynn Papers, Calendar of. 1930.

APPENDIX OF REFERENCES

CHAPTER I

APPROACH TO ENGLAND

[1] *Sorbière*, 3–8, 46–7, 54; *Cosmo*, 116, 202; *Rawlinson MSS.*, A. 172. ff 5, 113; 127, 133, 137, 139; *Statham, History of Dover*, 114; R. *Kilburne, Topography of the County of Kent.*
[2] *Sorbière*, 3–4, 7, 9–10; *Blundell*, 183; *Defoe*, 27, 122, 388; *Fiennes*, 194; *Traill*, IV, 664; *Verney Memoirs*, II, 311; *H.M.C. Portland*, II, 302–3.
[3] *Shakerley MSS.*; *Pepys* (21, 29 Jan., 2, 12 June 1661; 13 Feb. '63; 15 Sept. '65); *Wood, passim; Cosmo*, 398–9.
[4] *Sorbière*, 11; *Defoe*, 118; *Hasted, History of Kent*; R. *Kilburne, Topography of the County of Kent.*
[5] *H.M.C. Portland*, II, 279–81; R. *Kilburne, Topography of the County of Kent; Defoe*, 111–13, 114, 120, 125–6; *Fiennes*, 100; *Sorbière*, 11–12.
[6] *Sorbière*, 3; *Defoe*, 104.
[7] *Rawlinson MSS.* A. 188, ff. 114–19; *Fiennes*, 99; *H.M.C. Portland*, II, 276; *Defoe*, 94–5, 101–3, 123, 349–51; *Cosmo*, 197; *Sorbière*, 12; *H.M.C. Dartmouth*, III, 3.

CHAPTER II

THE CAPITAL

[1] *Bell, Fire*, 11, 17; *Cosmo*, 396; *Traill*, IV, 654; *Sorbière*, 15; *L.T.R.*, V, 126; *Pepys* (21 March, '63); *Defoe*, 316–18, 324; *Brown*, I, 202; *Thurloe*, II, 670.
[2] *Bell, Fire*, 11–12; *Misson*, 39; *Pepys* (29 April '63); *H.M.C. Cowper*, II, 427; *Ward*, 26; *Butler, Hudibras*.
[3] *Bell, Fire*, 8; *H.M.C.*, VIII (House of Lords, 157); *Cosmo*, 401; *Misson*, 30, 39; *H.M.C. Verney*, 469; *Pepys* (15 Dec. '62; 6 Feb., 13 June '63; 26 Oct. '64; 12 Jan., 12 Nov. '66).
[4] *Pepys* (26 April '63; 1 July '67); *Hatton*, I, 60–1; *North, Lives*, III, 105–6.

APPENDIX

⁵ *Bell, Fire,* 12; *North,* I, 107; *Pepys* (20, 25 Oct., 27 Nov. '60; 7, 8, July '63; 30 April '66); *H.M.C. Portland,* II, 308; *H.M.C. Dartmouth,* I, 129.

⁶ *Brown,* I, 13; *Pepys* (30 Jan., 8 Nov. '60; 1 April ' 62; 26 July '63; 21 April, 28 Dec. '64; 28 Sept. '65; 5 Sept. '67); *Wood,* III, 68.

⁷ *Wynn Papers,* 357; *H.M.C. Cowper,* 411.

⁸ *Evelyn, Miscellaneous Writings; Bell, Fire,* 10; *Evelyn, Diary* (Jan. '84); *Wood,* II, 121, 298.

⁹ *Pepys* (22 Nov. '68; 23 April, 1 May '69); *A Hue and Cry after Pepys and Hewer.*

¹⁰ *Bell, Fire,* 11, 14; *Defoe,* 327; *Sorbière,* 11, 12, 19; *Verney Memoirs,* II, 191.

¹¹ *Bell, Fire,* 128–33; *Sorbière,* 17; *Dugdale, St. Paul's; Thurloe; Cal. Clar. MSS.,* II, 770; *Chamberlayne;* 193–6.

¹² *Bell, Fire,* 12; *Pepys* (22 June '63); *Sorbière,* 302; *Blundell,* 140–1; *H.M.C. Portland,* III, 269; *Dryden, Wild Gallant,* Act II, Sc. ii; *Verney Memoirs,* II, 197.

¹³ *Cosmo,* 402; *Brown,* III, 277; *C.S.P.D.* 1666-7, XII; *Pepys* (6 Jan., 22 June, 26, 27, 30 July, 17 Sept., 11 Nov. '60; 25 March '61; 16 Aug. '63).

¹⁴ *Defoe,* 327; *Wood,* II, 176, 230; *H.M.C. Hodgkin,* 300; *Wynn Papers,* 374.

¹⁵ *Defoe,* 334–7, 392; *L.T.R.,* V, 131; *Brown,* I, 110; *Bell, Fire,* 112; *Sorbière,* 13–16; *Ward, London Spy,* 130–1.

¹⁶ *Brown,* III, 33; *Defoe,* 345–7; *Brown,* III, 33; *Sorbière,* 14; *Cosmo,* 296; *Pepys, passim; H.M.C. Dartmouth,* III, 120; *H.M.C. Gawdy,* 186; *Ward,* II, 74; *Verney Memoirs,* II, 315.

¹⁷ *North,* I, 66; *Pepys, passim; Wycherley, Plain Dealer,* Act II, Sc. i; *Sorbière,* 62; *Brown,* III, 15; *Ponsonby, English Diaries,* 136; *Harleian Miscellany,* VI, 465; *H.M.C.,* 6 (*Ingilby,* 381).

¹⁸ *Defoe,* I, 333–4, 355–6; *Cosmo,* 297, 176; *Howell,* 24–6; *H.M.C. Dartmouth,* III, 1–3; *H.M.C. Portland,* III, 211; *Fiennes,* 260.

¹⁹ *Pepys* (12 April, 25 Aug., 4 Sept. '63; 21 Jan., 23 Aug. '64; 21 Dec. '68; 4 Jan., 23 Feb. '69); *Verney Memoirs,* II, 312; *Sorbière,* 45; *Brown,* I, 149, 152; *H.M.C. Fleming,* 21; *North,* I, 399; *H.M.C. Portland,* II, 275.

²⁰ *Cosmo,* 297; *Howell,* 14; *C.S.P.D.* 1662-3, 86; *Chamberlayne,* 203 *et*

seq.; *Hatton*, I, 231; *Newdegate, Cavalier and Puritan*, 239; *Thurloe*, II, 670; *Pepys* (2, 8 April '68).

[21] *Pepys* (2 Feb., 22 July, 14 Oct. '60; 13 April '61); *Tanner, Further Correspondence of Samuel Pepys*, 297; *Brown*, I, 148, III, 136–7; *Ward*, 50; *Cosmo*, 401; *Misson*, 21; *Sorbière*, 14.

[22] *Howell*, 13–22; *Pepys* (26 Dec. '60; 24–5 March, 18 May '61; 24 March, 8 Aug. '62); *Fiennes*, 247.

[23] *Pepys* (7 Dec. '61; 14 May '69); *Brown*, III, 136–43.

[24] *Cosmo*, 320; *H.M.C.*, VIII (*Corporation of Trinity House*, 251); *Pepys, passim; H.M.C.* V (*Sutherland*, 196); *H.M.C. Fleming*, 49; *North*, III, 27–32.

[25] *Traill*, IV, 658; *Pepys, passim;* A. Nicoll, *History of Restoration Drama; Wycherley, Love in a Wood*, Act III, Sc. ii; *Cosmo*, 191; *Sorbière*, 69; *H.M.C. Fleming*, 29; L. Hotson, *The Commonwealth and Restoration Stage; C.S.P.D.* 1660–1, 1661–2, *passim; De Witt, Lady of Lathom*, 283; *Evelyn, Diary* (26 Nov. '61; 5 Feb. '64; 18 Oct. '66); *Orrery, Letters*, I, 81; *Roscius Anglicanus.*

[26] L. Hotson, *Commonwealth and Restoration Stage; Pepys* (1 June, 21 Dec. '63; 19 Aug. '66; 27 May '67; *Brown*, I, 151; *Cosmo*, 316; *Sorbière*, 71–2.

[27] *Brown*, I, 105, 211, III, 44; *Cosmo*, 175, 303; *Sorbière*, 15; *Shadwell, Virtuoso; Traill*, IV, 660; *Pepys, passim; Evelyn* (2 July '61).

[28] *Dryden, Sir Martin Mar-All*, Act IV; *Patrick Gordon, Diary*, 85–6; *H.M.C. Rutland*, II, 21; *North, Lives*, I, 66, II, 237; *Shadwell, Humorists*, Act V; *Pepys* (29 May '62; 23 July '64; 13 March, 22 April '68).

CHAPTER III

THE UNIT OF LIFE

[1] *Fiennes, Travels; Chamberlayne*, 6–11; *Evelyn* (31 Aug. '54); *Jusserand*, 168; *Pepys* (11 April '61; 13 Oct. '62); *Shakerley MSS.* For a description of the countryside of Restoration England, see *H.M.C. Portland*, II, 263–314.

[2] *Diary of the Rev. Giles Moore*, Rector of Horsted Keynes; *H.M.C. Rep.* 6 (*Ingilby*, 375–6); *House of Lyme*, 266; *North, Lives*, I, 37–8, 175, 183; *Pepys* (23 Dec. '60; 14 July '67); *Savile*, 135–6, 165, 179; *Shakerley MSS.* (16 May '79).

[3] *Shakerley MSS.; Verney Memoirs*, II, 176, 316, and *passim; Blundell,* 85, 139, 240; *Dorothy Osborne, Letters.*

[4] *Shakerley MSS.; Verney Memoirs*, II, 177–8, 188; E. Godfrey, *Home Life under the Stuarts*, 113–25.

[5] *H.M.C. Stewart,* 137.

[6] *H.M.C. Rep. 8 (House of Lords),* 136.

[7] *Shakerley MSS.*

[8] *H.M.C. Kenyon,* 176; *Blundell,* 132; *Shakerley MSS.; Dorothy Osborne, Letters.*

[9] *Pepys* (15 Nov. '60); *Shakerley MSS.; H.M.C. Portland,* III, 371; *Verney Memoirs,* II, *passim.*

[10] *H.M.C. Portland,* III, 270, 273; *Shakerley MSS.; Dryden, Wild Gallant; Blundell,* 164; *Congreve, The Way of the World; Verney Memoirs,* II, *passim; H.M.C. Cowper,* II, 448–9.

[11] *Shakerley MSS.; Verney Memoirs,* II, *passim; Blundell,* 56–61, 133; *Wood,* II, 319–20; E. F. Ward, *Christopher Monck, Duke of Albemarle,* 84–6; *North,* I, 34; *H.M.C. Rutland,* II, 54; *H.M.C. Portland,* III, 319; *Todd, History of Ashbridge; Ponsonby,* 130; E. Godfrey, *Home Life under the Stuarts,* 229 et seq.

[12] *Shakerley MSS.; Verney Memoirs, passim; Blundell,* 45, 70, 79, 133; *H.M.C. Rutland,* II, 78.

[13] *Shakerley MSS.; Verney Memoirs, passim; H.M.C. Rutland,* II, 78; *Thurloe, passim.*

[14] *North,* III, 3; *Shakerley MSS.; Blundell,* 74, 151, 153, 310; *Verney Memoirs, passim.*

[15] A. Tuer, *History of the Horn Book; Godfrey, Home Life under the Stuarts,* 31–9; *Shakerley MSS.; H.M.C. Fleming,* 373; *Rawlinson MSS.,* A. 194, f. 263; *Ponsonby,* 12; *Evelyn; North,* III, 10–11; *Blundell,* 176–7.

[16] *H.M.C. Portland,* III, 364; *Shakerley MSS.; Verney Memoirs,* I, 91–2, II, 311, 318, 387; *Wynn Papers,* 419; F. Watson, *The Old Grammar Schools;* J. Sargeaunt, *Annals of Westminster School;* A. F. Leach, *A History of Winchester College; H.M.C. Kenyon,* 91–2.

[17] J. B. Mullinger, *The University of Cambridge,* Vol. III; Sir C. E. Mallet, *History of the University of Oxford,* Vol. I; *Cosmo,* 221, 231, 265; *Wood, passim; H.M.C. Portland,* II, 264, 285; *Sorbière,* 44; *Prideaux, passim; Shakerley MSS.; Rawlinson MSS.,* A. 189, f. 331; *H.M.C. Fleming,* 150, 161, 165, 166, 193; *Verney Memoirs,* II, 413–430;

Terrae Filius; H.M.C. Rep. 5 (Magdalene College, 483); North, III, 14; H.M.C. Lonsdale, 93–4.

[18] *Shakerley MSS.; Verney Memoirs, II, 274–313; Reresby, passim; Blundell, 135; H.M.C. Fleming, 374–9; Plot, Oxfordshire; Evelyn, Sylva; Evelyn, passim; H.M.C. Portland, II, 309; House of Lyme, 279–82 Kip, Britannia Illustrata; R. Blome, The Gentleman's Recreation.*

CHAPTER IV

RELIGIO MEDICI

[1] *Blundell, 108.*

[2] *Shakerley MSS.; Ponsonby, English Diaries, 129–30.*

[3] *Walker, Sufferings of the Clergy, passim; Cosmo, 130, 135, 153; Sorbière, 10, 17; H.M.C. Portland, II, 277; Traill, IV, 650; Defoe, I, 277–8; C. Cosin, Corr., II, 10; Jusserand, 120; Verney Memoirs, I, 486; II, 171.*

[4] *Sorbière, 17; Cosmo, 143, 400; Wood, II, 44; H.M.C. Gawdy, 195.*

[5] *Cosmo, 415–57; Defoe, I, 227; C. Walker, Compleat History of Independency; Reliqiae Baxterianae; D. Neal, History of the Puritans; E. Calamy, Historical Account of My Own Life; O. Heywood, Autobiography.*

[6] *Traill, IV, 496; Wood, II, 1; Brown, I, 10; H.M.C. Leeds, 15–16; Wynn Papers, 385; H.M.C. Fleming, 58; Baxterianae 231 et seq.; Ponsonby, English Diaries, 132.*

[7] *Sheffield, Duke of Buckingham, Memoirs, I, 15.*

[8] *Kennet, Register, 296; H.M.C. Kenyon, 157; H.M.C. Fleming, 31–2; Fox, Journal, passim; Josselin, Diary, 112; Kennet, 288, 296, 356, 364; Thurloe Papers, III, 693; Brown, I, 107.*

[9] *Prideaux, I; Wood, II, 228; G. Sitwell, First Whig, 95 et seq.; Hatton I, 119, 157; Williamson, I, 85; Ailesbury, Memoirs, 27; Evelyn (4 April '72; 25 Aug. '78); H.M.C. Dartmouth, III, 24–5.*

[10] *Cosmo, 404; Blundell, 71, 80–1, 172–7, 234; Sir C. Duckett, Penal Laws and Test Act; Bedingfield Papers; R. de Courson, The Condition of English Catholics under Charles II; M. V. Hay, The Jesuits and the Popish Plot.*

[11] *Muddiman, King's Journalist, 131–3; H.M.C. Portland, III, 268–9, 354; Wood, II, 24, 88; Ponsonby, English Diaries, 155; H.M.C. Eglinton, 57.*

APPENDIX

[12] *Verney Memoirs*, I, 175, 223, II, 129–33, 295–6, 383–4, 473–4; *Pepys* (20 Jan. '60; 7 July, 22 Aug. '61; 23 Dec. '63); *H.M.C. Kenyon*, 79, 99; *Ponsonby, English Diaries*, 137; *Wynn Papers*, 396; *H.M.C. Rep. 6 (Ingilby*, 369); *H.M.C. Egmont*, II (27 Nov. 1669).

[13] A. H. Buck, *The Growth of Medicine; Brown*, III, 89; *Wood*, II, 95, 308; *Raymond Crawford, Last Days of Charles II.*

[14] *Ponsonby, English Diaries*, 116; *Verney Memoirs*, II, 300; *H.M.C. Gawdy*, 208; *Fiennes*, 8; *Blundell*, 57–60; *H.M.C. Portland*, III, 239, 313; *North*, 1, 45; *Wood*, II, 122; *Godfrey, Home Life under the Stuarts*, 230–1.

[15] *The Periodical*, Oct. 1927; *H.M.C. Gawdy*, 200; *Evelyn* (15 Sept. '85); *H.M.C. Portland*, III, 292–3; *Shakerley MSS.*

[16] *Tho. Sydenham, Works*, I, 213; *Verney Memoirs.*

[17] Sir *D'Arcy Power, An Historical Lithotomy; Evelyn* (24 March '72); *Carte MSS.*, 73, f. 325; Sir T. Longmore, *Richard Wiseman, Memorials of the Craft of Surgery in England* (ed. Sir D'Arcy Power).

[18] *Englishmen at Work and Play; Celia Fiennes, Travels*, 11–17, 22, 24, 83, 109; *H.M.C. Portland*, II, 314, III, 346, 372; *Defoe*, I, 157, 160–1; *H.M.C. Rep. 3 (Northumberland*, 93).

[19] B. Allen, *The Natural History of the Chalybeat and Purging Waters of England; Englishmen at Work and Play; Brown*, I, 77; *H.M.C. Portland*, III, 372; *Pepys* (13 June '68); *Fiennes*, 11–17.

CHAPTER V

HABIT AND PASTIME

[1] *H.M.C. Portland*, II, 291, 314; *North*, III, 3; *Wynn Papers*, 405.

[2] *Wood*, II, 97, 399; *Pepys, passim; H.M.C. Cowper*, II, 411; *H.M.C. Portland*, II, 263–5, 295, 299, 306–7, 312; *Cosmo*, 403; *Traill*, IV, 670; *Brown*, I, 152; *Fiennes*, 8; *H.M.C. Dartmouth*, I, 138.

[3] *H.M.C. Dartmouth*, I, 6; *Wynn Papers*, 410; *Verney Memoirs*, II, 215; *Blundell*, 236; *Pepys* (13 Dec. '60; 17 July '67); *Defoe*, I, 152; W. Hughes, *The Compleat Vineyard; Chamberlayne*, 10.

[4] *Verney Memoirs*, II, 315; *Wood*, II, 96; *North, Lives*, I, 64–66; III, 30, 108, 171; *H.M.C. Portland*, II, 293; *Prideaux*, 32–5; *H.M.C. Hodgkin*, 17; *Evelyn* (18 March '69); *H.M.C. Rutland*, II, 52; *Jusserand*, 97; *Lady Newton, House of Lyme*, 271; *H.M.C. Ormonde*, IV, 18; VII, 278.

180

APPENDIX

[5] *Pepys, passim; Ward, London Spy,* 42; *Dryden, Wild Gallant,* Act I, Sc. i; *Shakerley MSS.; Traill,* IV, 671; *H.M.C. Portland,* II, 312; *Defoe,* I, 509; *Pepysian MSS.,* No. 2867, 416.

[6] *H.M.C. Portland,* II, 295, 318; *Fiennes,* 156, 159–60, 164, 177, 218; *Cosmo,* 396; *Blundell,* 65.

[7] *Bradley, English Housewife; R. May, The Accomplisht Cook. Teonge, Diary; Pepys, passim.*

[8] *Pepys, passim; Traill,* IV, 668–9; *Cosmo,* 377–8; *Bradley, English Housewife; Blundell, Cavalier,* 100; *Wood,* III, 84; *Godfrey, Home Life under the Stuarts.*

[9] *Rules of Civility,* 138–41; *Pepys* (19 June '63); *Cosmo,* 324, 350.

[10] *Sorbière,* 62; *Cosmo,* 464; *Rules of Civility,* 122–45.

[11] *Cartwright, Madame,* 137; *Evelyn, Diary* (1 March '71); *Grammont, Memoirs,* I, 144–5; *H.M.C. Rep.* 6 *(Ingilby,* 368); *H.M.C. Rep.* 8 *(Portsmouth,* 91); *H.M.C. Buccleuch* (M. H.), I, 427; *H.M.C. Fleming,* 191.

[12] *Rules of Civility,* 20, 21, 61–4, 99, 109, 118–20; *Cosmo,* 166; *Rawlinson MSS.,* A. 194, f. 244; *T. Smith, Life, Journals and Correspondence of Samuel Pepys,* II, 229–30.

[13] *Rules of Civility,* 75, 107–8, 144–50; *Cosmo,* 193, 378–80.

[14] *Wood,* II, 332; *H.M.C. Rep.* 6 *(Ingilby,* 367); *H.M.C. Hamilton,* 149–50; *H.M.C. Wombwell,* 135.

[15] *Add. MSS.,* 25124, f. 43; *Gallus Castratus, passim; Jusserand, passim; H.M.C. Rep.* 2 *(Mount Edgcumbe,* 21); *H.M.C. Rep.* 7 *(Verney,* 465, 470; *Lowndes,* 575); *H.M.C. Ailesbury,* 170; *H.M.C. Fitzherbert,* 25; *H.M.C. Fleming,* 62–3, 70; *H.M.C. Rutland,* II; *Reresby, passim; Pepys* (27 Nov. '60; 18 April '61; 27 March, 26 July '64; 3 March '69).

[16] *Hatton,* I, 66, 119–21, 158; *H.M.C. Rep.* 2 (Spencer, 21–2), *Rep.* 4 (Rogers, 405–6), *Rep.* 5 (Sutherland, 159, 168, 177), *Rep.* 7 (Verney, 465, 469–60, 473, 478, 479–81, 484, 494), *Rep.* 8 (House of Lords, 101, 122); *H.M.C.* (Bath, II, 160); *H.M.C.* (Dartmouth, I, 75; Fleming, 62, 121; Kenyon, 116; Montagu of Beaulieu, 182; Ormonde, V, 281, VI, 117; Portland, III, 320; Rutland, II, 11, 17, 24, 27, 43–4, 62); *House of Lyme,* 245; *Newdegate,* 72–3, 78; *Nicholas,* IV, 263; *Pepys* (1 Feb. '64); *Reresby* (Sept. '60; 4 July '61; 12 July '63; July '66; 19 March '78); *Verney,* II, 314–15, 320–1; *Williamson,* I, 41–2, 86–7; II, 89–90.

APPENDIX

¹⁷ *Sitwell, First Whig*, 95; *Hatton*, I, 119, 157; *Newton, House of Lyme*, 259–60; *Williamson*, I, 85; *Jusserand*, 144.

¹⁸ *North*, I, 37; *Defoe*, I, 154–5; *Pepys* (11 Aug. '61; Sept. '67); *Shakerley MSS., Dryden, Wild Gallant*, Act III; *H.M.C. Cowper*, II, 394; *H.M.C. Fleming.*

¹⁹ *Wynn Papers*, 397; *H.M.C. Salwey*, 414–15; *Shakerley MSS.* (Aug. 1665); *H.M.C. Portland*, II, 299; *H.M.C. Cowper*, II, 409; *R. Blome, The Gentleman's Recreation; Pepys* (21 March '66).

²⁰ *Evelyn* (22 July '70; 17 Dec. '84); *H.M.C. Rep.* 6 (*Graham*, 338), *Rep.* 7 (*Verney*, 488); *Finch*, I, 266, 290; *H.M.C. Kenyon*, 84; *H.M.C. Fleming*, 56; *H.M.C. Leeds*, 9; *H.M.C. Portland*, II, 265, III, 314; *H.M.C. Russell-Astley*, 30; *H.M.C. Rutland*, II, 15; *Josselin, Diary*, 159; *Jusserand*, 162; *Savile*, 115; *Cosmo*, 205–16; *Defoe*, 75–7; *Verney*, II, 462; *J. P. Hore, History of Newmarket.*

²¹ *Wynn Papers*, 357; *I. Walton, The Compleat Angler; Blundell*, 357; *Cosmo*, 209; *Shakerley MSS.; Pepys* (April 1660).

²² *H.M.C. Rep.* 6 (*Ingilby*, 365); *D'Urfey, Songs; Strutt, Sports and Pastimes of the English People; H.M.C. Corp. of Kendal*, 316; *Ponsonby, English Diaries*, 123; *Pepys* (3 Jan. '65); *J. Marshall, Annals of Tennis, Chamberlayne*, 57–8.

²³ *H.M.C. Braye*, 180; *Fiennes*, 16; *North*, III, 9.

²⁴ *North*, I, 20–21; *H.M.C. Kenyon*, 67; *Dryden, Wild Gallant*, Act I, Sc. i; *Pepys* (2 Jan., 15 May '60; 17 Feb. '62); *The Compleat Gamester.*

²⁵ *Pepys, passim; H.M.C. Rep.* 6 (*Ingilby*, 373); *North*, I, 320, 339, III, 67–88; *Memoirs of Musick; Reresby* (6 July '66); *H.M.C. Portland*, II, 307; *Wood*, II, 4; *Sir F. Bridge, Samuel Pepys Lover of Music.*

THE MEANS OF LIFE

¹ *G. N. Clark, The Seventeenth Century*, 9; *Traill*, IV, 649; *Chamberlayne*, 53; *Gregory King.*

² *Traill*, IV, 650, 653–4; *Gregory King; Shakerley MSS.; North*, I, 31; *Chamberlayne*, 6–10.

³ *Traill*, IV, 652–4; *Defoe*, I, 100, 131; *Cosmo*, 219; *Shakerley MSS.; Rogers; Blundell*, 41, 100; *North*, I, 31; *Fiennes*, 135; *Verney Memoirs*, II, 177, 195–6; *J. Blagrave, Epitome of the Art of Husbandry; A. Varranton, The Great Improvement of Lands by Clover; J. Forster,*

APPENDIX

England's Happiness Increased; Lord Ernle, English Farming Past and
Present; The Countryman's Treasure.

[4] Shakerley MSS.; Traill, IV, 652-4; H.M.C. Fleming, 365, 367; Blundell,
passim; H.M.C. Portland, II, 280, 282; Defoe, I, 430; Rogers.

[5] Rogers; Shakerley MSS.; Defoe, I, 531; Fiennes, 4; Wynn Papers, 392;
H.M.C. Fleming, 369, 388; Blundell, 71; H.M.C. Gawdy, 204-6;
H.M.C. Portland, II, 307.

[6] Cosmo, 200, 244; Evelyn (31 Aug. '54); Defoe, I, 14, 81, 447-8, 451, 550;
Fiennes, 158; H.M.C. Portland, II, 270, 304.

[7] Fiennes, 133; Cosmo, 147, 201; Defoe, I, 53, 68-9, 129, 284-6, 394,
447, 471.

[8] Defoe, I, 218, 290, 430, 488-9; Cosmo, 147.

[9] H.M.C. Portland, II, 275-6, 283, 309; Defoe, passim.

[10] Shakerley MSS.; North, I, 19, 42; Pepys (19 Feb. '64); Blundell, 119.

[11] G. N. Clark, Seventeenth Century, 10-12, 17; H.M.C. Portland, II, 266,
295, 303, 310, 328; Cosmo, 133; Shakerley MSS.; Evelyn, Diary.

[12] Sorbière, 12, 46; H.M.C. Rep. 8 (House of Lords, 135); H.M.C. Rep. 9
(House of Lords, 8); Brown, I, 213, II, 24; H.M.C. Portland, II, 275-6;
Fiennes, 176; Defoe, I, 130, 229-31; Tanner, Catalogue of Pepysian
MSS.; H.M.C. Dartmouth, I, 4; C.S.P.D. 1660-83, passim.

[13] Traill, IV, 654; H.M.C. Portland, II, 270, 283, 304, 310; Defoe, I, 18,
66-7, 141, 189, 221, 279-83, 441, 448, 550, 600-14; Cosmo, 133;
Fiennes, 207; H. Heaton; The Yorkshire Woollen and Worsted
Industries; J. Burnley, History of Wool and Wool Combing; Rawlinson
MSS., A. 189, f. 29.

[14] Defoe, 13-14, 125, 141, 238, 435-6, 440-1, 467-8, 565; Wynn Papers,
359; H.M.C. Portland II, 272-5, 281, 294; Traill, IV; Norden;
Brown, I, 213; H.M.C. Rep. 8 (House of Lords, 134-5); C.S.P.D.
1660-83, passim.

[15] H.M.C. Lonsdale, 96; H.M.C. Kenyon, 87; Shakerley MSS.; H.M.C.
Portland, II, 291, 298, 300, 309; Defoe, 156, 269, 458, 590; Traill,
IV, 648; Pepys (1 March '67); Reresby; H.M.C. Rep. 9 (House of
Lords, 9); Fiennes, 132; J. Parkes, Travel in England in the Seventeenth
Century.

[16] J. Parkes, Travel in England; H.M.C. Portland, II, 302-3; H.M.C.
Kenyon, 83; Shakerley MSS.; Pepys (20 Sept. '63); Fiennes, 7, 9,
11, 32, 66, 116, 128, 159, 169, 189, 197, 216; Defoe, 129, 493, 517,
521, 523; Blundell, 79, 183.

APPENDIX

17 *Cosmo*, 202; *Brown*, I, 137; *Fiennes*, 128, 185; *H.M.C. Portland*, II, 267, 289, 290, 292–7, 300, 303, 305, 308, 310.

18 *Shakerley MSS.; Sorbière*, 44; *Wood*, II, 221–3; *Brown*, I, 211; *Blundell*, 192; *Defoe*, 215, 227.

19 *Shakerley MSS.; Traill*, IV, 663–4; *Blundell*, 104, 155; *C.S.P.D.*, *passim*; *H.M.C. Fleming*, 43; *Verney Memoirs*, II, 294; *The Present State of London*, 345–59.

20 *Shakerley MSS.; Defoe*, 84, 289, 292.

21 *Account of Several Late Voyages and Discoveries*, 1694; *Ady* (14 Sept. '68); *Ailesbury*, 97; *C.S.P. Colonial* (*America and W. Indies*, 1661–81) Preface; *C.S.P.D.*, 1662–3, 184; *Cunningham, Industry and Commerce*, II, Pt. 1, 198–202; *Echard*, 1041; *Evelyn* (18 Dec. '82; 2 Feb. '83); *H.M.C. Dartmouth*, III, 5; *H.M.C. Downshire*, I, i, 5; *Fleming*, 72, 87, 102, 126, 128; *Middleton*, 195; *Rutland*, II, 62; *Hunter, British India*, II, 185; *Luttrell* (9 June '81; 1 June '82); *Reresby* (March '83); *Verney*, II, *passim*; *Wood*, II, 71, *H.M.C. Portland*, III, 262.

22 *Evelyn*, *passim*; *North*, II, 291; *T. Sprat, History of the Royal Society*, 53–4, 93, 133, 158–82, 190–213, 215–40, 246–51; *Williamson*, II, 7; *Petty Papers*; *T. Birch, History of the Royal Society*.

23 *Evelyn* (7 Sept. '60; 9 March '61; 10 July '67); *H.M.C.* (*Beaufort*, 49–50; *Hodgkin*, 175–6); *North, Lives*, I, 153–4, 320, 387–93, 434, II, 243–5, III, 63–6, and throughout; *Pepys* (4 March '64; 14 March '68); *Plot, Oxfordshire*, 227 *et seq.*

24 *Brown*, III, 86–7; *Ward*, 17; *Sorbière*, 32–3, 35–7, 47; *North*, III, 26; *H.M.C. Beaufort*, 49.

25 *Cosmo*, 396; *Pepys* (5 June '67); *Defoe*, 112, 123; *Wood*, II, 89; *H.M.C. Fleming*, 364 *et seq.; North*, III, 34; *Traill*, IV; *Cunningham*.

26 *Rogers; Shakerley MSS.; Traill*, IV, 654; *H.M.C. Portland*, II, 278, 295, 310; *Wood*, II, *passim*; *H.M.C. Fleming*, 23, 27, 367; *Wynn Papers*, 410.

27 *Rogers; Shakerley MSS.; H.M.C. Portland*, II, 297; *Wood*, *passim*; *H.M.C. Fleming*, 21, 367, *et seq.; H.M.C. Rutland*, II, 68.

28 *Rogers; Shakerley MSS.; Wood*, *passim*; *Cosmo*, 253, 266; *H.M.C. Fleming*, 22, 29, 381.

29 *Pepys*, *passim*; *Shakerley MSS.; Wood*, *passim*; *Blundell*, 61, 64, 72, 94, 99; *H.M.C. Somerset*, 109; *H.M.C. Fleming*, 22, 368, 371; *H.M.C. Rutland*, II, 77; *Traill*, IV, 664–6; *Dryden, Wild Gallant*,

APPENDIX

Act I, Sc. i; *Rules of Civility; Wynn Papers*, 421; *Ponsonby;*
H.M.C. Rep. 6 *(Ingilby* 367); *H.M.C. Portland*, II, 210; *Forneron*,
161.

CHAPTER VII

THE ENGLISH POLITY

[1] *Chamberlayne*, 155–90 *et seq.; H.M.C. Ormonde*, II, 2–5; IV, 642 *et seq.*
VII, 185; *Rochford, Travels; Sheppard, Whitehall, passim; State
Papers Dom.* lxxvi, f. 67; *Cosmo,* 368; *Sorbière*, 17.
[2] *H.M.C. Rep.* 6, 364; *Rep.* 7 *(House of Lords,* 88–92); *Pepys* (27 Oct.
'62; 13 April '66; 6 Oct. '67; 5 Jan. '68); *Williamson*, I (8 Aug. '73);
Cosmo, 369.
[3] *Ailesbury*, 93; *Essex*, I, II, *passim; Reresby* (Sept. '60); *Teonge, 203.*
[4] *Ailesbury*, 15, 85; *C.S.P.D.* 1661–2, 350; *Essex*, I, 280; II, 33; *Evelyn*
(14 May, 3 Oct. '61; 13 Sept. '66); *H.M.C. Rep.* 5 *(Sutherland,*
199); *H.M.C. Ormonde*, IV, 277, VII, 27–31; *Newdegate*, 23, 27.
[5] *Ailesbury*, 93; *Chamberlayne*, 207–9; *Evelyn* (23 April, 3 Aug. '67);
Halifax, 203–4; *Lauderdale*, III, 28; *Pepys* (11, 25 July '66; 8 Sept.
'67; 4 April '68); *Reresby* (29 Nov. '81). See also *H.M.C. Buccleuch*,
II, 105.
[6] *A. Amos, The English Constitution in the Reign of Charles II; Chamberlayne,
Angliae Notitia; Cobbett, Parliamentary History*, Vol. IV; *Clarendon,
History of the Rebellion; Commons Journals;* E. *Coke, Institutes of
the Laws of England; Eachard, History of England; K. Feiling, History
of The Tory Party;* S. R. *Gardiner, Constitution Documents of the
Puritan Revolution: History of England; Grey, Debates;* H. *Hallam,
Constitutional History of England; Harleian Miscellany; H.M.C.
Rep. (House of Lords);* G. B. *Hertz, English Public Opinion after the
Restoration;* W. S. *Holdsworth, History of English Law; Lords Journals;*
F. W. *Maitland, Constitutional History of England;* C. H. *Mellwin,
The High Court of Parliament;* D. J. *Medley, Student's Manual of
Constitutional History;* J. *Nalson, The Common History of King
and People; Old Parliamentary History; Ponsonby*, 142; E. *and* A. G.
Porritt, The Unreformed House of Commons; G. W. *Prothero, Select
Statutes; State Tracts; Ranke, History of England;* G. M. *Trevelyan,
England under the Stuarts;* E. *Wingate, The Body of the Common Law;
English Historical Review*, Vol. XXI (W. C. *Abbott, The Long Parlia-*

ment of Charles II); W. Notestein, The Winning of the Initiative by the House of Commons.

[7] *E. Trotter, Seventeenth Century Life in the Country Parish; S. and B. Webb, English Local Government: The Parish and the County, Vol. I; Englishmen at Work and Play; Shakerley MSS.*

[8] *Shakerley MSS.; C.S.P.D.* 1663–4, 219; *Somerset Quarter Sessions' Records,* I, 36; *Reresby, passim; Cosmo,* 378, 396–9; *Pepys* (28 Sept. '60, 12 April '69); *North,* I, 30; III, 108; *Wood,* II, 11, 115, 313, 341; *H.M.C. Rutland,* II, 11; *H.M.C. Kenyon,* 88; *Sorbière,* 7, 46–7, 50, 54; *Rawlinson MSS.,* A. 194, f. 268.

INDEX

187

INDEX

Whitehall, 41, 44, 53, 114, 159-61, 163, 164; *see also* Court, the
Wiltshire, 132, 138
Winchester College, 71
Windsor, 117, 117n, 171
Withington, 144
Wood, Anthony, 77, 80, 94, 114, 158
Woolwich, 25, 42

Worcester, 101, 140
Worcestershire, 102
Wren, Sir Christopher, 150, 151
Wye, River, 132

Yare, 132
York, 24, 112, 145
York, Duke of (*later* James II), 40
Yorkshire, 98, 101-2, 137, 139, 141

DATE DUE

JUL 19 '64			
OCT 28 '64			
DEC 12 '64			
MAR 14 '65			
JUN 20 '69			
JUN 20 '69			
OCT 29 '78			
DEC 13 '78			
DEC 14 1994			
MAR 22 '99			
GAYLORD			PRINTED IN U.S.A.